More Food From Small Spaces

Growing Denser, Deeper, Higher, Longer Gardens

Margaret Park

☙ Great River Books ☙

Salt Lake City

For information contact:

Great River Books
161 M Street
Salt Lake City, UT 84103

www.greatriverbooks.com

Library of Congress Cataloging-in-Publication Data

Park, Margaret, 1954-
More food from small spaces : growing denser, deeper, higher, longer gardens /
Margaret Park. -- 1st ed.
    p. cm.
 ISBN 978-0-915556-42-7
 1. Vegetable gardening. 2. Small gardens. 3. Square foot gardening. I. Title.
 SB321.P355 2013
 635--dc23
                                    2012044879

Printed in the United States of America   10 9 8 7 6 5 4 3 2 1

Contents

Preface

A few years ago our family put an addition on the back of our house, and in the course of construction, most of the grass and plantings in our backyard were destroyed. We were faced with the task of designing our backyard from scratch. This was not an unwelcome development. There had not been much aesthetic sense or maturity to the backyard landscaping we'd inherited from the previous owners. Our house is very close to downtown in a good-sized American city. Needless to say, its dimensions are very limited, especially after the addition was completed. I have always loved gardening, and especially loved growing flowers, ornamental plants and creating peaceful outdoor resting spaces. My husband is fond of building rock walls and paths, so our

thoughts naturally turned to creating a serene and beautiful oasis in the city. Then in 2008 with economic downturn and the ensuing stagnation, our dreams of a peaceful oasis in the city, turned toward another kind of peace — the greater security of knowing we could grow a lot of our own food.

Now, we are glad we chose this direction. The cost of food has steadily risen and our income has not followed apace. This is a familiar story for many of us. And if you have picked up this book because you're feeling financially pinched, I want to assure you that even if you have just a small patch of dirt available to you — even as little as 8 x 16 feet — you can grow a lot of your own vegetables and save money, especially with current food prices and the likely prospect of future price increases.

Using these savings for other purposes every month will seem a great reward for your garden labors. As for a beautiful backyard, we've found that vegetable gardening in such a small space demands that order and structure be emphasized. At this scale, our vegetable garden has its own charm and exudes a vibrance and abundance that looks close enough to beautiful for our tastes.

Over the years, through various moves across the country, I've grown vegetables on a number of different properties. My prior vegetable garden in a rural area was 25 x 30 feet. I've now learned how to grow more food in my current 8 x 24 foot plot than I used to grow in three times this space. Over the last four years I've experimented and figured out how to make small space gardening work. And now I think I've got it! To express these discoveries in as few words as possible: you have to plant denser, deeper, higher for longer. It's all about cramming as many plants as possible into an alloted space for a longer part of the year and the vertical supports and soil fertility that enables this tight grouping to flourish.

This book is essentially a how-to guide that includes all the information you'll need to grow your own vegetable supply: from how to maintain soil fertility to how to cut and snap together inexpensive, durable plant towers out of pvc plastic pipes and pipe connectors. I also show how to make a portable/storable greenhouse that will add months of life and harvesting to your vegetable garden.

This is not meant to be a comprehensive book on the technical and scientific aspects of vegetable gardening. I do not delve deeply into soil composition and technical matters of plant growth. There are many fine books that present more fully researched technical information than what I offer here. I am motivated to write this book because I've been consistently successful with the methods I offer and have come up with some original solutions that I don't believe are offered elsewhere. In fact, I've been amazed at how much food we now grow in our tiny urban backyard. These ideas will be of most use to the urban and suburban gardener, but even rural home vegetable growers may appreciate the many advantages to keeping the garden small. Less space means less work, especially for the initial setting up of the vegetable patch. Small spaces require less weeding and watering. Large vegetable gardens require walking pathways that need weeding and maintenance as much as the planting beds. Water, especially in mechanically watered spaces, is often wasted in watering pathways. Hand watering a large space is a lot more time consuming than a small space.

The money savings is only one of the rewards of planting a garden. It's no secret that the activities involved in growing vegetables can be deeply satisfying. Gardening is one of the most popular hobbies in America. There's something inherently inspiring about the great benevolence of plant life in our wide and interconnected world. Becoming a part of this ongoing, seamless whole by placing some seeds in the ground and caring for them as they grow makes us nurturers as well as consumers. It's so ultimately trusting and optimistic and grounding to plant, not to mention the natural pleasure of being outside in sunshine and fresh air. It seems basic to our human nature to care for the things that are destined to become part of us.

Growing up in Brooklyn New York, I remember the backyard gardens I could view from the rear windows of my parents' railroad apartment three stories up. Cultivating vegetables in New York City seemed

very foreign and old fashioned to me then. Actually, it was foreign, since the vegetable gardens were mostly planted by immigrant families extending their cultural values and cuisines into this new country. Living in this ethnic neighborhood, I saw vegetables in yards that never could be seen in the local supermarkets. I suppose that's why people grew them. I only later in life learned the names of kohlrabi, arugula, and trombetta squash. Now, growing food is not at all foreign to me, it's become an all around nautral and pleasurable activity.

I believe there are great benefits for our health in eating what the garden provides. When we've grown the food ourselves, we know exactly what's gone into the growing process. We can avoid the toxic pesticides and herbicides that are often applied on commercially grown crops. We can avoid the genetically modified plants that are more and more being introduced to consumers. We can select the varieties of seeds we want to plant. We can even choose heirloom, open pollinated seed varieties and collect our own seeds for future crops.

Will our home grown food be more nutritious? This is a question that is harder to answer. Like with so many topics, it's hard to come to a general conclusion through the scientific studies. The results of studies that compare the nutrient content of organically farmed versus conventionally farmed foods fall on both sides of the question, so there's no consensus about whether organically grown food has a higher nutrient load. Soil quality and amounts of sunshine and watering can vary greatly, so it is difficult to compare findings of different studies. But, what would we rather eat; food grown without the use of herbicides and pesticides or conventionally grown food?

As a home gardener you will have control over the factors that lend nutritional quality to your vegetables. Soils can be tested and amended through mineral supplements and other natural additives. You can avoid pesticides and other chemicals. You can be sure that the food you eat is uncontaminated by harmful organisms like salmonella or e-coli bacteria. You can choose the varieties you prefer based on your conditions, harvest at peak ripeness, and consume your produce at maximum freshness. It will be all under your control.

Peak maturity and freshness ensures that you're eating food with all the final sugars and nutrients in place. Certain sugars, called glyconutrients, are very important for the body's cell communication, thus immune system. Harvesting fruit and vegetables before they are ripe, as is commonly done with commercially grown food, can mean less nutrition because it's only in the last few days of the ripening process that the plant puts important glyco-nutrients into the fruit or vegetable. And aside from the questions of nutrition, the flavor of just picked food is unsurpassed and it is probably still embued with vital life force.

We now grow most of our own vegetables in our diminutive, urban backyard. Our roughly 8 x 24 foot patch of ground yields nearly all the vegetables a small family can eat for almost ten months out of the year. In our climate zone, our fresh vegetable harvesting more or less ceases from late December through late February. It was such a surprise to me that such gardening success could be accomplished. It is the reason why I am writing this book. We can do so much for the health of our bodies and finances and feel a little more secure and empowered in our future. If all else fails in our lives, at least we can eat some healthy home grown vegetables and feel a little more independent.

My own goal of greater food security was achieved by optimizing a few significant gardening factors. I planted the vegetables densely, encouraged them to grow up instead of out, sowed seeds repeatedly through the year and extended the life of plants through colder seasons with simple effective techniques. This book will show you how to include all of these ideas and techniques in your own garden, as well.

1

Denser

The Center Square Plan

This book focuses on getting as much yield as possible out of a little plot of ground. In addition to planting densely and often, it's also crucial to not waste space by growing foods we're simply not going to eat. One summer we grew a beautiful section of okra plants, and I do mean beautiful with their striking yellow and purple flowers resembling hibiscus and the okra pods arranged on the branches like candles on a candelabra. However, we never got around to eating a single okra, and could have used more carrots in the fall.

Since our backyard is so small, I decided to sacrifice convenience for more plantable square footage. It's always seemed a waste to have a lot of walking paths in the vegetable garden. From the beginning of my planning, I came up with the idea of the central square system to maximize my space. Garden bed dimensions have to be limited to the human wingspan. In order to weed and take care of the plants, not to mention harvest the food, you need to be able to reach all spots in the beds. You also don't want to walk on the soil and compress it. Plants don't fare well when their soil is compressed. Their roots need air permeating the soil, and roots spread more easily in looser soil material. It's difficult to manage maintenance and harvesting when the crop beds are more than four feet wide, and they can only be four feet wide if you can get around the sides of the bed. So, that's the limit — with a four foot wide bed it's easy to cultivate the areas within two feet of you.

In my initial planning, it occurred to me that I could cultivate an eight foot square area and be able to work all parts of it, if it had a central working area. I knew I would also need to be able to reach in from outside this eight foot square area, so I really needed some walking space around the perimeter of the footprint as well. I discovered that with a two foot wide working area in the center I could reach all areas of the bed and I could even place another eight foot square area with its

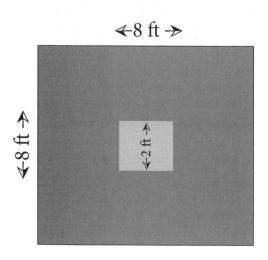

own central square next to it and be able to cultivate the areas in between from one central square or the other. I have found that this arrangement is the best for maximizing the planting beds in a small garden plot. Compare the following garden plots to see how much more efficient this design is than four foot wide beds with walking paths in between.

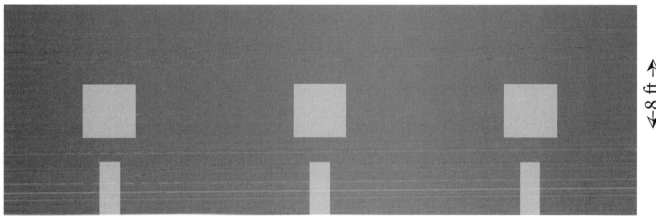

Approximately 177 square feet of planting beds

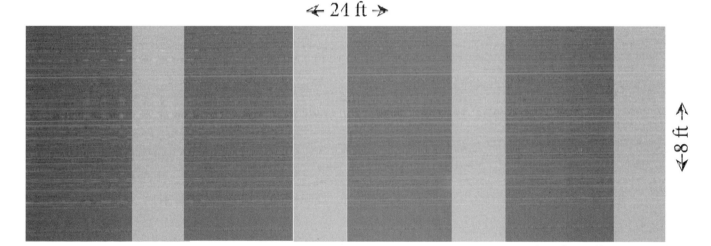

Approximately 128 square feet of planting beds

The center square plan has approximately 49 more square feet of growing soil in the same sized footprint.

A bit more of a reach is needed in the areas between the central squares, so if you're not able to reach every spot in the soil, make your central area more rectangular so that you can reach every spot. This will still give you more space for planting than putting in full walking paths. The reulting bed dimensions are also big enough to carve into multiple smaller sections for adequate crop yields of multiple plant varieties.

8 x 8 foot garden section with center square

Heat retaining lava rock warms the
air from the center square

Benefits of the Center Square

There are other benefits that the center square space provides. The square can be filled with heat retaining rock, such as lava rock to add warmth to the late fall and early spring plantings. Heat from the sun shining on the rocks in the central square will be absorbed during the day and retained a little longer after the sun goes down, especially when covered in the evening with a garden cloth. To really maximize this effect, lava rocks can be heated with enhanced solar energy (in a later chapter I show how to construct a simple solar heating arrangement that can be used as an oven for cooking or as a food dehydrator.)

In hotter weather, basins of water can be placed on the central square to cool the air and increase moisture in the air around the plants on hot summer days. When water evaporates, heat is removed from the surrounding surfaces. A good emergency way of cooling is to wrap something that needs to stay cool in a wet cloth or newspaper and place it in the sun. The process of evaporation removes heat calories from the cloth and keeps the object cool. The moisture in the air and natural cooling will benefit nearby plants in hot, dry weather. When temperatures are too hot, plant fruit production may shut down and a crucial period for potential tomato production can be lost. Later we'll talk about other ways to cool the garden but the centrally located basin of water is facilitated by having these open working squares within the vegetable patch.

Bowl of evaporating water cools the air from the center square

Garden Siting

The number of hours of sunlight has to be a consideration in choosing the site for a vegetable garden. Most vegetable plants need at least six hours of sunshine a day. Before choosing, take a few days to familiarize yourself with the light conditions in the yard. Look at nearby trees and structures like buildings and fences. A garden with a long side on the south is best. If your southern exposure is situated on the shorter width of your plot, then having the longer length opening out to the west is the next best choice. When planting flowers and shrubs western exposures are considered full sun conditions, eastern exposures are considered part shade conditions. We have our vegetable garden close to a fence on the northern border of our yard. Since our yard is so very small, we've only left about twenty inches between the fence and the vegetable patch. It's cramped for working on that side of the garden, but it's enough. This walkway is bare dirt that we keep free of weeds, but it's also not a bad idea to leave a lawn mower width strip of grass for walking and working on. If you do have a grass border, bury a weed barrier between the grass and the vegetable plot. Plastic, fiberglass, or metal edgings can be bought at garden centers. Brick or stone can be used. Many materials will work if they can be buried five or so inches deep to prevent grass roots from moving into vegetable beds.

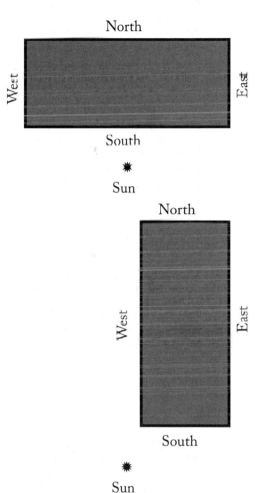

There are also advantages to building a slightly higher frame around the plot. The frame provides a container for the soil. It's a distinct boundary that pets and small children can be trained to respect. The frame is also something that can keep out unwanted pests if you dispense discouraging materials around the outsides. It should not be so high that it impedes your ability to reach into the garden beds.

We have very many snails in our area that can and have utterly decimated the young seedlings of many a crop. Snails seem to love all the food we humans love to eat. They can set back your garden many

Cute, but annoying backyard competitor

weeks if you fail to remove them. A few years ago an internet search about snail control yielded the interesting tidbit that snails can't come into contact with copper without causing damage to their underbellies due to a chemical reaction. We found some leftover pieces of copper flashing, cut them into strips and nailed them to the top of the wooden boards surrounding our garden. It's possible that this helped a bit, we seem to have fewer snails in our garden than other people in the area, but I lose a lot of faith in this method when I witness a snail casually sliding over the copper strips not seeming at all in distress.

In chapter six, I discuss some other non-lethal pest repelling measures, but slugs and snails are especially determined creatures. I find that an evening snail patrol is the best strategy for discouraging snails, especially when the weather is wet. If I see a snail, I just pick it up and banish it to another part of the yard. Slugs are a little harder to pick up without harming, but they can be maneuvered onto a bit of cardboard and moved away. This is another virtue of a small garden space. My snail patrols don't take long at all. And since the garden space is mostly free of weeds, I can spot the snail invaders heading toward the seedlings. Most mature plants can handle a little snail nibbling. The seedling stage is when the snails inflict the most garden damage. Please don't kill these interesting little beings, they are living creatures that simply want to eat and they deserve our mercy.

How to Build a Border

Stacked 2 x 4s for more height

You can use cedar or redwood if you want the borders to last longer, but these will be more expensive and may not be worth the investment. Ordinary two by fours or two by sixes, bought new, or leftover from other projects will last quite a number of years. These days, metal two by four studs are becoming more available and these may be a cheaper, more durable choice for bordering the vegetable garden. What you really shouldn't use are pressure treated boards that are prepared with poisonous chemicals such as: chromate copper arsenate, ammoniacal copper arsenate, and ammoniacal copper zinc arsenate. These pressure treated boards should not be used near animals or food crops. Railroad ties are treated with creosote, which has been found to be carcinogenic. These poisons can leach into the soil and be taken up by plant roots.

If you would like a higher border, two by fours can be stacked one on top of the other. Grounding stakes can be cut longer to join the stacked wood at several places along the length and at seams and corners. Make sure these stakes are of sufficient length to anchor the border in the ground.

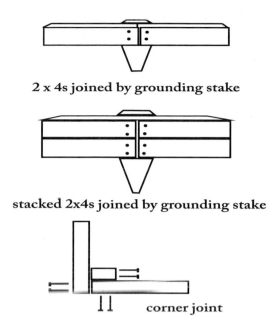

2 x 4s joined by grounding stake

stacked 2x4s joined by grounding stake

corner joint

stake anchoring the border

Framing Around the Center Square

The central square area can be left as an unbordered section of soil or it can be lined with bricks, pavers, flagstones or one big stepping stone. Sooner or later, with all these choices, the soil of the square area will become compacted from standing and working on it. This can become a problem when the soil surrounding the square (where you do want to plant) begins to slope into the square draining water away from the planting beds. For this reason, it is good to create a solid border of wood or brick around the square to maintain level soil beds outside the border.

back yard deck as a border

Which Vegetables to Choose

Earlier I mentioned our untouched okra crop of a few summers ago. This is a cogent example of how not to plant—not that I'm discouraging the planting of okra. Okra is a wonderful, unique vegetable that has recently been found helpful in reducing cholesterol. The vegetables you eat the most should be at or close to the top of your list of what to plant. Next I suggest you give a nod to those vegetables that are better and tastier than their store-bought counterparts and easy to grow. Surely tomatoes are at the top of this list, but other good ones are leaf lettuces and mesclun lettuce mixes. Home grown spinach is delicious

**Wood border around
the central square with
large stepping stone**

and a lot easier to clean than most store bought spinach. Sugar snap peas are a wonderful treat that can be planted early, harvested early and cleared away early to make way for another crop. Following are some of my personal home grown vegetable ratings.

Better Tasting and Easy to Grow in the Home Garden

Arugula	Beet	Cucumber
Eggplant	Green bean	Kale
Leaf lettuce	Okra	Pepper
Radish	Spinach	Sugar snap pea
Summer squash	Swiss chard	Tomato
Turnip	Winter Squash	Zucchini

Following are plants that I don't find as valuable in the home vegetable garden. I am not discouraging growing them, but they are less successful for me than the varieties above. I do grow many of them anyway, because we eat them so often.

Parsnips can have difficulty germinating and take many months to mature

Harder to Grow or Not Always Superior to Store Bought

Broccoli	Cabbage	Carrot
Cauliflower	Celery	Corn
Fennel	Head lettuce	Parsnip
Pea	Potato	

Corn and potatoes especially require a lot of space and are fairly inexpensive to buy. Peas are not difficult to grow when planted in early spring. They're on this list because small space gardeners will get more food value from edible podded peas. Parsnips can have difficulty germinating. Broccoli, cabbage, cauliflower, head lettuces, and celery can take a lot of time until they reach their harvestable stage. Home grown carrots are rarely as sweet as store bought carrots.

Broccoli can take many months to mature

My approach to onions, garlic, annual herbs, and radishes is to intersperse them between other compatible plants. For instance, basil grows quite nicely in the space in front of tomato plants.

If you take a look at your allotted space for growing these vegetables and begin to doubt whether you can really grow all the vegetable varieties you want to try, remember that you can successively plant crops year-round and have the time and space to try them all.

Companion Planting

Companion planting is something to be aware of in planning where your vegetable varieties will grow. Certain vegetables tend to deter insects and pests that may infest other vegetables and others can actually enhance the growth of their companions. Companion planting is a fascinating subject and there are many online sources of information to learn about and test. In my small space, however, I seldom have the luxury to both crop rotate and site plant companions fully, so I have taken the approach of learning which plant varieties tend to actively interfere with one another in order to avoid these combinations. Following is a list of incompatible plant neighbors.

Don't plant onions or garlic near beans or peas.

Don't plant dill or parsnips near carrots.

Don't plant strawberries, tomato or dill near cabbage

Don't plant potatoes near cucumbers

Don't plant pungent herbs near cucumbers

Don't plant sunflowers, cucumbers or tomatoes near potatoes

Don't plant cabbage, fennel, or potatoes near tomatoes

Actually, there isn't much that likes to grow near fennel!

There are a couple of helpful plants that you may want to reserve space for in your yard simply because they enhance conditions for other plants in the garden. Borage is a beneficial companion for most plants, but particularly for tomatoes, squash and strawberries. Borage discourages pests like tomato hornworms and cabbage worms and attracts beneficial insects like bees and wasps. Borage in the compost bucket adds trace minerals to the soil. It's self seeding and has edible flowers.

Comfrey is a perennial plant that sends its roots very deeply into the soil to build its very mineral-rich leaves. Adding its leaves to a compost bucket improves the soil, or a tea can be made from the leaves to be used as a foliar spray for the plants. Place comfrey leaves in a covered container and immerse them in water to cover. Allow this brew to stand for a couple of weeks – two weeks in hot weather, four weeks in cool weather. The tea can be added to the soil around plants. To use as a spray, collect all the "tea" (squeeze the leaves to expel even more liquid). Add water in the proportions of $1/3$ cup of comfrey tea to one gallon of water. Place in a spray bottle to feed the leaves of your vegetable plants.

Lower height plants on the south side. Taller plants and plant towers on the north side

Marigolds, especially the scented varieties, discourage nematodes and insects when planted densely. Whiteflies cannot tolerate them. Don't plant marigold near beans or cabbage, but I have had success planting them near tomatoes.

Planting Guide

Plant your shorter vegetables on the south side of the garden and your taller ones on the north side. If the long sides of your garden are on the east and west, then plant shorter plants on the west side and taller ones on the east. This will prevent the larger plants from shading the smaller ones.

When to Plant

It is good to know the traditional last frost date for your area to know when it's safe to sow seeds or set out plants that cannot withstand a frost. An internet search for your area will probably unearth this information. Local agricultural or university extension offices will also have this information. In January 2012, the Department of Agriculture unveiled a new plant hardiness zone map that shows generally warmer low temperatures for winter than the department's previous map from 1990. Your area's last frost date may be a few weeks earlier than previously recorded.

Indoor Seed Starting

Following are some varieties you may want to start indoors with artificial lighting or perched on sunny windowsills. There are several good grow light arrangements available that allow you to start seedlings many weeks in advance. The nightshade family of plants, i.e. tomatoes, peppers and eggplants are good candidates for indoor starts. In many U.S. climate zones, if you wait until after the last frost to sow these nightshade varieties directly in the garden, you risk not getting any fruits before the first fall frost. Other candidates are below.

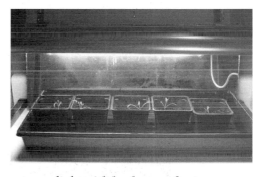

growlight with background mirror to
amplify the light

Vegetable	Weeks before last frost
Chives, leeks, onions	12
Celery	10
Eggplant, Peppers, Tomatoes	8
Broccoli, Cabbage, Cauliflower	6
Cucumbers, Squash	3

When starting seeds in pots, the soil should be loose and free of weed seeds. You can buy seed starting soil at garden supply stores that are generally mixtures of peat moss and vermiculite or perlite. I have been disappointed by these formulas and have started to use my own garden soil in the seeding pots. My garden soil is loamy and well developed, so it is suitable for seed starting. If you have loamy soil and want to use it for seed starting, following is a good method to eliminate weed seeds that may be in the soil.

Push the soil through a screen – quarter inch hardware cloth is suitable to use, though a finer mesh would be even better. Then heat the sieved soil to 180 degrees to kill any weed seeds. This heating can be done in your home oven or in a solar cooker.

Greenhouse Seed Starting

In chapter four, I show how to make a simple, 6 x 8 foot portable greenhouse. If you decide to make one, you can get a much earlier start to your garden. Many seeds can be started directly in the soil in the greenhouse to either complete their growth in place or to be transplanted elsewhere. If you save your own seeds you will have plenty of seeds to spare and will be able to risk earlier greenhouse starts.

Cabbage family plants (cruciforms) can be planted in the greenhouse anytime between autumn and early spring. Root vegetables can also be started from fall to early spring. However, if using the greenhouse to start root vegetables (beets, carrots, turnips, parsnips), it is better to wait to sow the seeds until a week or two after the winter solstice. If sown before, the plants may not make their big bulbous roots before choosing to go to seed. On the other hand, since I prefer turnip greens to turnip roots, planting in the fall has been a good no-guilt strategy for getting a lot of greens.

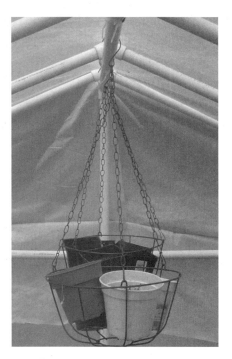

Starting seedlings out of harm's way

The nightshades can be planted in the greenhouse about eight weeks before the last frost date. These you will most likely be transplanting, though some you may wish to leave in place. If snails or slugs are entering your greenhouse, you can protect your nightshade seedlings by starting them in hanging baskets and suspending them from the ridgepole of the greenhouse. Cucumber and squash family seeds may also be started in the greenhouse or indoors ahead of time, but you will only save two or three weeks — if that — since transplanting will set back their growth as well. Unless you have a great deal of well-lit indoor growing space or room in the greenhouse, I recommend cucumber and squash seeds be started in their outdoor place after the last frost date. More information on greenhouse seed starting will be found in chapter four.

Hardy Plants to Directly Sow Before the Last Frost Date

Following is a general chart showing the vegetables that can be planted directly in the soil before the last frost. All of the following can also be started in a greenhouse between autumn and early spring.

Vegetable	Weeks before last frost
Peas, Spinach	8
Broccoli, Cabbage, Cauliflower, Kale, Kohrabi, Turnips, Mustard	6
Beets, Carrots, Chinese Cabbage, Endive, Radish, Swiss Chard	4

Tender Plants to Directly Sow After the Last Frost Date

Vegetable   **A week or two after last frost**

Beans, Celeriac, Corn, Cucumber, Melons, Squashes

Plant Spacing

With good soil fertility, vegetables can be planted very densely to increase your yield in a given area. The plant spacing ideas you'll find here makes this method different from many other growing guides.

If you are new to gardening, planting in lines will help you distinguish between your sprouted vegetable seeds and random weeds that may germinate. You can rest assured that weeds will never line up to sprout. If you are unfamiliar with the look of the various vegetable seedlings, it may be handy to arrange your seeds in straight lines in your first garden, especially if you anticipate weeds. Otherwise, planting in staggered grids will allow adequate, yet closer spacing for the seeds.

Some Common Vegetable Seedlings

lettuce

beet

carrot

kale

parsnip

spinach

turnip

For ease of planting, I suggest you construct a simple seed planting grid to guide the placement of seeds in the soil. You can use an old picture frame and tie strings from side to side at two-inch intervals across the width and the length. If you prefer something more durable, you can drill holes every two inches in the sides of the frame and lace wire through the drilled holes from side to side to create the grid.

 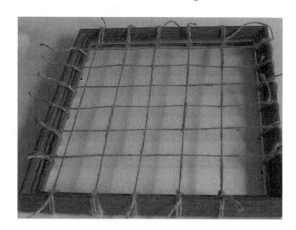

Varieties to Be Sown in Every Two Inch Grid Square
Arugula, Radishes,

	X	X	X	X	X	X	X	X	X	X	X	X
	X	X	X	X	X	X	X	X	X	X	X	X
↞ fourteen inches ↠	X	X	X	X	X	X	X	X	X	X	X	X
	X	X	X	X	X	X	X	X	X	X	X	X
	X	X	X	X	X	X	X	X	X	X	X	X
	X	X	X	X	X	X	X	X	X	X	X	X
	X	X	X	X	X	X	X	X	X	X	X	X

← twenty-four inches →

Varieties to Be Sown Every Other Square, Staggered

Beet, Carrot, Leaf Lettuce, Parsnip, Spinach, Turnip, Bean, Chard

X		X		X		X		X		X	
	X		X		X		X		X		X
X		X		X		X		X		X	
	X		X		X		X		X		X
X		X		X		X		X		X	
	X		X		X		X		X		X
	X		X		X		X		X		X

← twenty-four inches →

sixteen inches →

Varieties to Be Sown Every Fourth Square (six inches apart)

Brussels Sprouts, Cucumbers, Chili Peppers, Okra, Kohlrabi, Kale

X			X			X			X		
X			X			X			X		
X			X			X			X		

← twenty-four inches →

fourteen inches →

25

Varieties to Be Sown About Twelve Inches Apart

Broccoli, Cabbage, Cauliflower, Bell Peppers

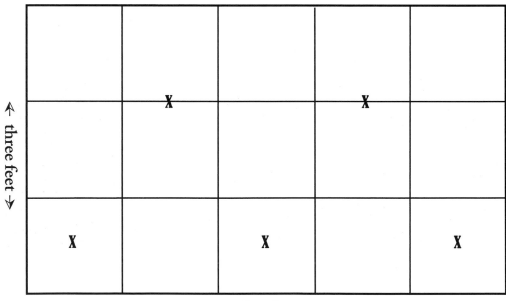

← five feet →

Varieties to Be Sown About Eighteen Inches Apart

Tomatoes, Eggplant, Zucchini, Summer and Winter Squashes

← five feet →

When using the planting grid, place it on the prepared soil and mark every grid square you plan to use by creating an indentation in the soil with a stick. Place at least two seeds in each marked grid square and bury the seeds to the appropriate depths. Most seed packets recommend a planting depth for the type of seed inside. When in doubt, use a one quarter inch depth for lightweight seeds and one half inch depth for heavier seeds.

When all the seeds in a grid area are planted, move the grid over to the next contiguous area and repeat the planting steps. If multiple seeds per grid square germinate, thin to one plant each when the seedlings are three or four weeks old. At this stage of growth it should be easy to tell which seedling is stronger or in a better position. If there are gaps in the sproutings, it's better to sow a few more seeds than try to transplant the plants you have culled. In my experience, they rarely thrive.

Beets every other two inch square staggered

Okra every fourth square — six inch spacing

Bell Peppers twelve inches apart

Tomatoes eighteen inches apart

Harvesting

It matters when vegetables are harvested. Root vegetables have the best flavor when young and tender. Once they start to go to seed,

**pick okra and zucchini
when young and small**

**pick beans, cucumbers, and eggplants
when young and tender**

**pick green peppers
when large and fleshy**

the tubers turn woody and inedible. Cucumbers, summer squashes and peas are also best tasting when small and firm. Okra should be carefully watched and picked when small and tender—it doesn't take long from flower to harvestable pod. It's easy to tell when to pick a tomato or a red pepper. Zucchini and eggplants are tasty in small or large, though overripe eggplants can be bitter, so pick earlier unless you're saving a specimen for seed collection. Bell peppers can be harvested when green and a little immature, but they will be sweeter when more fully mature.

In general, the winter squashes should be left on the vine until after a frost when the plants place their final sugars into the fruits. A Hubbard squash is ready when your fingernail can't leave a mark in its skin. Melons are probably the most difficult to judge (this holds for choosing ripe ones at the supermarket too.) Cantaloupes are ripe when gently sliding your thumb against the vine will easily separate it from the fruit. They also have a strong fruit odor when ripe. Watermelons are ready when they sound hollow when you knock on them.

Pick often the vegetable varieties that have seeds inside, such as tomatoes, peas, cucumbers, beans, etc. to encourage the plants to produce more. Plants do want to reproduce themselves as seeds. and may keep on trying as you harvest their fruit or seed pods.

2

Deeper

The Fertile Soil Base for Intensive Planting

This system of densely planted crops requires soil with excellent structure and nutrient load to sustain the packed-together plants. Care to the soil extends to the food that will grace your table with nutritional density, as well. In this chapter, we'll be talking about the initial big dig to aerate the soil. Later in the chapter, you'll learn a wonderful, easy composting method that quickly builds and maintains good soil, no matter the condition in which it starts out. Our own backyard soil started out as compacted, concrete-like dirt that was loaded with small stones. It was difficult to stick a shovel in, especially when dried out, as it tended to be in summer. Within a year, it became rich and loamy and is now (four years later) populated with many earthworms. The other gardens I've dug in my life have not been nearly so much work to start, so please don't be pessimistic about your soil, because it can be transformed and become the foundation for great and high quality food yields.

One year I experimented with the method of planting in soilless raised beds. It sounded so easy. Forsake the native soil — dirt in many cases — and fill an area enclosed with boards with loose and fertile mixtures of peat moss and composts. I built three 3 x 6 foot raised beds on some unused space next to our driveway. It was a test to compare with the yields of identical varieties of vegetables I was growing in the backyard native soil beds. Though the raised beds were pretty easy (but expensive) to construct and to fill with 6 inches of soil, the produce they yielded was disappointing, especially in comparison to the yields from my backyard vegetable plot. Corresponding plants were one-third to one-half the size of the backyard plants. The yields in number of vegetables were similarly, much, much less. The only plants that did pretty well were the tomatoes (though their yields were less than half the number of my backyard tomatoes). The root vegetables, chard and

Tomato plants in a raised bed of twelve inches of a soilless growing medium grew barely three feet high

Tomato plant nearly reaching the top of a five foot tomato tower

other nightshades I planted were very disappointing. Cucumber plants in the raised beds yielded two cucumbers each. My backyard cucumbers were prolific. The following year I decided to double the depth of the raised beds to twelve inches, and planted carrots and beets, but they were miniscule. I've spoken with a number of people that had similarly disappointing results with their raised beds. I suspect that the beds simply get too hot and dry. Another drawback to the raised bed method is the resultant environmental destruction of peat bogs around the world. The soil in raised beds usually relies on peat moss to fill out the soilless medium. Peat bogs are being mined and rapidly depleted, yet the bogs can only slowly restore themselves.

Raised beds may be necessary for people who have physical difficulties bending and kneeling in a garden, but I don't recommend them for greater yields. If you have no other option than using the raised beds and you want to grow a few vegetables you may be satisfied with the method, but if you want to grow most or all of your vegetables, I recommend you use your native soil. There are always ways to amend and improve soils, but this does take some initial work.

Digging Deeply and Doing It Once

The first step after choosing the site of your vegetable plot is to double dig the soil. This will loosen it and provide an opportunity to layer in compost as you go. Digging aerates the soil allowing oxygen to penetrate through. While plants mainly grow on carbon dioxide fuel for their sugar production, roots and the microbes that feed those roots need oxygen. Plant roots rely on microorganisms to turn inorganic soil minerals into more bioavailable versions that they can take up.

Admittedly, double digging a patch of soil is a lot of work, but there is good news. If you never tread on your vegetable beds, you'll only have to dig them deeply once.

When is the best time to till your soil? Have you heard the answer to the old question; When is the best time to plant a tree? Answer: twenty years ago. And the next best time? Today.

If your soil isn't frozen and you want to start eating those great tasting, free vegetables, then get busy. This being said, it sure is nice to time this outdoor work for early spring when it's warming up and it's so inspiring and invigorating to be outside. I always love the return to the dirt after a long winter spent mostly indoors. However, anytime the soil is unfrozen you can start digging. Another good point about spring cultivation is the soil is generally moister and easier to spade after spring rains. If the weather has been very dry and your soil is hard and dry, soak it well with a hose and dig it up a few days later when it's no longer muddy and soggy. There are certain clay soils that will respond to your shovel blows like kiln fired brick—let the water work its magic.

Fall is also a good time to begin the garden. You can at least start to cultivate an 8 x 8 foot soil bed for the greenhouse area. Then in early spring you can cultivate more space next to it.

Tap with a trowel to loosen dirt

Removing Sod

If the plotted area is covered with grass or a ground cover of plants or weeds, remove the grass and all the roots. Shake out loose soil from the roots over the plot. If you have space in your yard for composting these grass clumps, then place them in plastic garbage bags, sprinkle in cups full of the bokashi compost accelerant you'll learn about later in this chapter and close the bag. The bags can be stacked one on top of the other to save space. In a couple of months or so, (depending on the temperature) you'll have some very nice compost to add to the garden soil.

Shoveling

Digging up soil is not a brain bender and one's shoveling technique is not a crucial factor for garden success. What is important is not injuring yourself by digging in an unbalanced way. When shoveling, be mindful of the proper body mechanics for lifting other kinds of heavy weight. This means lowering your stance by keeping your knees bent and keeping your center of gravity within an imaginary cylinder close to your body. In short, don't extend heavy shovelfuls of dirt too far from your torso if you don't want to strain your back muscles. Be aware of when your muscles are getting fatigued and rest for awhile.

The soil should be dug down at least eighteen inches, but twenty-four is better. Twenty-four inches is roughly two shovel blade lengths, hence the popular term double digging. If you are planning to add an initial load of compost or other amendments to the soil, place these on top of the soil before beginning to shovel. The amendments will mix in as you work along.

Work systematically for greatest efficiency by digging trenches that you can later walk in while digging the next trench. If you have a plastic tarp available, it helps to lay it down outside the perimeter of the plot and alongside the first trench to be dug. You can deposit the soil from the first trench onto the tarp and add it back later into the

place the first row of dirt on a tarp outside the digging area

vegetable plot. Then move along the plot filling the last trench with dirt from the new trench being dug.

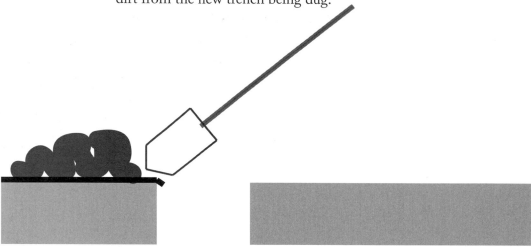

Dig out a first trench, depositing the soil on a plastic tarp outside the vegetable bed area

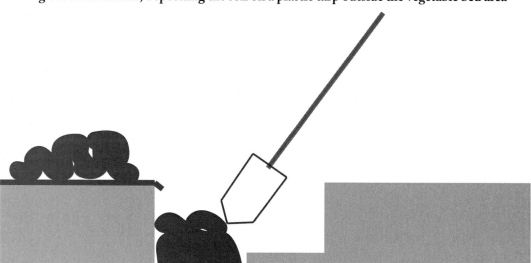

Dig out the next trench, depositing the soil in the previously dug out trench

Removing Rocks

Rocks are sources of minerals and perhaps even sources of subtle earth energy, so it's not necessary to take out random small stones in the vegetable garden. My husband and I faced a real ordeal when we first dug up our vegetable garden and it took us a very long time to accomplish this phase. Our back yard was once at the bottom of an ancient lake. The dirt was literally like concrete, not much more than dust interspersed with zillions of tiny stones. In dry weather, we could not heave a shovel into the dirt more than half an inch. It had to be broken up with six-foot long iron bars to loosen it enough to lift out the dirt. We constructed a rectangular sieve out of old two by four boards covered with ¼ inch hardware cloth (a closely spaced metal grid) that we ran our shovelfuls of dirt through. Most backyard soils I've encountered are not like this. However, if you feel you also need to construct such a sieve, don't make it so big that it can't be lifted up to pour off the rocks. And if you have access to a wheel barrow, make the dimensions so that the sieve can span over the wheelbarrow sides, but not so big that soil will fall outside the wheelbarrow. 30 x 34 inches is ideal. If your dirt is easy to dig, count yourself lucky. We slaved over our vegetable plot and I have to say, four years later, it was well worth it. Besides, we used the stones we dug up to make attractive paths around the yard.

**2 x 4s held together with 90°
angle hardware and covered
with hardware cloth**

After this initial digging is the best time to install a garden border and the border around the central square. The soil level will be raised from the aeration it's received and you'll know how high to construct the borders. If you don't ever walk on your soil, you will not have to till like this again. You'll only be digging up the soil to add compost to it.

Enriching the Soil

Most states have an agriculture extension service with information about the area's soil and climate conditions for growing vegetables. Many locales even offer inexpensive soil analysis tests for residents. These usually involve requesting soil sample boxes from the agriculture extension agency (sometimes they are connected with local universities) and sending in some soil samples from your yard. Testing will tell you if your soil has any particular deficits that need correcting and what to add to improve its quality.

**The sieve's dimensions are customized
for use with a wheelbarrow**

Adding Mineral Content

In general, adding rock dusts to the soil will enhance the mineral content of the foods we grow. Our bodies require dozens of essential vitamins and minerals to keep us in good health. Control of our soil quality is one of the biggest benefits of home gardening. We know our plants will have excellent nutrient loads if we've added minerals to the soil ourselves. It is a very good idea to just go ahead and re-mineralize the soil in your vegetable garden with mined mineral products that contain many trace minerals important to our diets that may be deficient in backyard soils. Following are some products you can find online that can be added to boost the mineral content in your soil. I have had favorable results using Azomite and Humic Shale. These products are not chemical fertilizers, but rather naturally mined materials that provide a diversity of minerals. Chemical fertilizers generally add only nitrogen,

Path made with dug out stones

potassium and phosphorus to the soil. Rock dusts can add dozens of beneficial minerals and elements. They can be added to the surface of cultivated soil and gently worked in. Adding one or another of these rock dusts every year or two will feed your plants well and help ensure that the food you grow provides excellent nutrition.

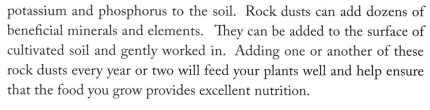

According to the producer's website: "Azomite® is a mined natural mineral product. For over sixty years, livestock and crop producers have utilized this unique material from central Utah to improve livestock and plant growth. Analyses reveal that the material contains a broad spectrum of over 70 metabolically active minerals and trace elements. Azomite® requires no mixing. It is odorless, will not burn plants and will not restrict aeration or water penetration. Unlike some products, Azomite® is not a manufactured, chemically prepared fertilizer. It is 100% natural with no additives, synthetics or filters. "

Greensand is a naturally occurring mineral mined from ocean deposits from a sedimentary rock known as Glauconite. It is often an olive-green colored sandstone rock found in layers in many sedimentary rock formations. Greensand forms in anoxic (without oxygen) marine environments that are rich in organic detritus and low in sedimentary inputs.

Typical chemical constituents of Greensand

Iron	12 - 19%
Potassium	5-7%
Silicon	25%
Oxygen	45%
Magnesium	2-3%
Aluminum	1.9%
Sodium	0.27%
Hydrogen	0.47%

Over 30 other trace minerals and many micronutrients.

Humic Shale is another mined product that can be added to boost soil mineral content. It has a dust-like consistency that can be spread on the soil and worked in with a hoe. During the earth's prehistoric era, our topsoil was incredibly rich with humic and fulvic acids. Plants were able to absorb high concentrations of minerals and grew to immense sizes being full of minerals and life giving nutrients. Layers of these old forest floors are mined to produce Humic Shale. It's not rock. It's not fossilized. It's just a layered, compacted deposit of plant life that never fossilized or petrified. Since it's made of plants, it's obviously composed of all the nutrients a plant uses. They grow strong and healthy when supplied with it.

Composting with Effective Microorganisms

Generally, I add these "rock" amendments once a year, but what I supply continually and plentifully to my garden is my own composted garden and kitchen waste using a simple composting system accelerated with Effective Microorganisms (EM). I attribute most of my gardening success to this simple composting system that makes lots of usable compost quickly and inexpensively. As an added benefit, I dispose of a lot less trash for the city pick-up than I used to. I stand in awe of what these little beneficial microbes have done for my soil. Of course, all composting methods eventually rely on microorganisms for breaking down materials, but the great advantage of the Bokashi EM system is the speed and simplicity with which you can build soil. All you need is the Bokashi accelerant, (which you can prepare at home) two buckets – an actively collecting bucket in your kitchen and a fermenting bucket outdoors – and whatever plant peels, stems, leaves, etc. you wish to dispose of as valuable fertilizer for your soil. There's no need for piles, bins, drums or other equipment to take up outdoor space that could otherwise be used for growing plants.

These microorganisms consume and break down the kitchen waste. They also convert soil minerals into more bioavailable versions. Though a lot of plant nutrition comes from photosynthesis in the leaves, plant roots are also consuming the byproducts of microorganisms. This is where our nutrient dense food comes from. Earth minerals and organic materials are converted by microorganisms into usable food for plants, which we later consume.

Making Your Own Bokashi for Composting

The combination of microorganisms known as EM were discovered by Japanese scientist Dr. Teruo Higa while he was working at the University of Ryukyus, in Okinawa Japan in 1982. One day he spilled some microorganisms on the ground and a few days later noted that shrubs near the spill site had grown disproportionately and were looking very healthy and vibrant. He began testing different microorganism blends until he came up with the best combination of beneficial microorganisms. Eventually, he introduced EM™ as a soil conditioner.

Dr. Higa's EM formula is a combined culture of aerobic microorganisms (requiring oxygen to survive) and anaerobic (requiring no oxygen to survive) that co-exist together to the mutual advantage of both, in what's known as symbiosis. These organisms also enhance the microorganisms within the soil to work together to build healthy soil.

Microorganisms play many roles in the environment. We humans, for instance, could not survive without the friendly microorganisms in our guts that help us break down the food we've eaten. In the microbial world there are the bacteria that are beneficial to us and there are the pathogens that can cause disease and pollution. Research on the EM cultures has shown that these friendly microorganisms can suppress soil-borne pathogens, accelerate the decomposition of organic wastes, increase the availability of mineral nutrients and useful organic compounds to plants. The EM organisms enhance the activities of other beneficial microorganisms, as well, e.g., mycorrhizae, nitrogen fixing bacteria, etc. reducing the need for chemical fertilizers and pesticides. EM is not toxic or pathogenic and is safe for humans, animals and the environment. It increases beneficial soil microorganisms and suppresses harmful ones.

Most organics, including animal manures and composts, have populations of microorganisms. Many of these are beneficial upon introduction to the soil, however, they can soon be overwhelmed by the existing soil microorganisms. Thus, the beneficial effects of microorganisms introduced with the application of composts are often short lived. With EM, however, the beneficial microorganisms are in much greater numbers, and in optimally balanced populations when introduced, so they remain dominant in the soil for a much longer time.

Space Saving and Plentiful Compost with EM Bokashi

We can make compost by various methods, but being realistic about who the "we" is, we should give credit to where it is due. Decomposition is a completely natural activity of nature's microorganisms. We humans can speed up this process and we can select the space where it happens, but the actual work is performed by the microbes. One way to "make" compost is to simply pile up waste material somewhere, but this will take up a lot of space, look messy and probably attract some local vermin. It also might take several years to get anything usable with this method, so various means to speed things along have been devised. There are bins and tumbler-like collection containers, rules and procedures for layering different kinds of waste materials (dry and wet) in these collectors. You can't simply throw waste in a bin and expect to speed things up. I collected dry plant clippings and even wet kitchen waste in a big black composting bin before I started making the EM bokashi compost. Finally, after three years of decay, there was a layer of compost about 10 inches deep at the bottom of the bin. In that same three years, I'd made 150 to 180 gallons of bokashi compost, roughly five gallons a month.

I will not go into the procedures for layering compost materials in a bin here, because I feel there is no better system than the EM bokashi method. In my experience, it's the easiest, cheapest, most space saving, most efficient way to make plentiful compost quickly -- and it all happens in just two lidded buckets. One bucket can be kept in your kitchen for collecting kitchen waste. The other bucket can be kept outside for a few weeks of additional fermentation. I recommend the outdoor bucket be about twice the volume of the indoor bucket. That way, you're moving older waste out of the kitchen faster. My indoor bucket is two gallons and my outdoor bucket is five gallons. I can dump two loads into the outdoor bucket and by the time the third kitchen bucketful is ready to move out, the five gallon outdoor bucket is ready to be buried.

An outdoor bucket about twice the volume of the indoor one

It's nice if the buckets, especially the outdoor bucket, has a tap at the base to drain accumulated liquids from the decomposing process. Keeping the bucket drained of liquid will keep odors at bay. However, this is more a nicety than a necessity. The EM microbes in the bokashi medium help keep down the populations of more odorous microbes. In fact, EM microbes are often employed to clean up polluted sites and in animal pens because of their odor fighting capacity.

Using bokashi turned our backyard garden plot from dead, dry dirt to living healthy soil nicely populated with worms and microorganisms in about a year. When we were digging up our concretized dirt we despaired of ever having earthworms plowing through our soil. We dug an 8 x 24 foot area two feet down and saw very few worms in the course of those digging sessions. We were later surprised at how quickly the worms did reproduce and believe this population growth was due to our bokashi composting. The rotting wastes provided plentiful microorganisms for feeding both worms and plant roots.

So what is EM bokashi? It's a mixture of a dry organic material inoculated with activated Effective Microorganisms. Wheat or rice bran is most commonly used because the grains of bran are small and they easily mix with the liquid EM. Bokashi can also be made of finely chopped hay or sawdust, or mixtures of any or all of the above. There are sources online for buying ready made bokashi that you can intermittently sprinkle onto the waste in your kitchen bucket, every day or so. Or you can make your own bokashi.

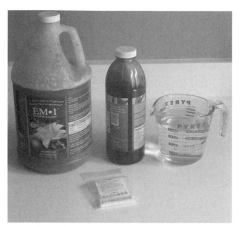

EM, molasses, water, pH strips

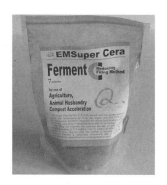

Optional ceramic powder

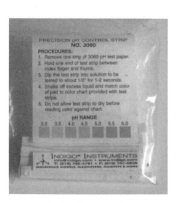

Pack of pH strips

Making Your Own Bokashi

Making Bokashi is a two step process. First, you have to activate the Effective Microorganisms with water and molasses and bring this mixture to the proper pH of 4.0 or less. This activated brew is used to make the bokashi mixture, but it doesn't have to be made every time you need to make more bokashi. The activated EM brew will last for many months stored in an airtight jar at room temperature. In fact, I have used year-old activated brew and it worked just fine.

In the second part of the process, you mix the activated low pH brew with bran and a few other things. In this two step process, it will be three to four weeks before any bokashi is ready.

Directions for Activating the Effective Microrganisms

You will need:

A bottle of EM-1, which you can buy online. (Buy the smallest amount available. It will last a long long time)

Ceramic powder (an optional ingredient)

pH strips – they should be able to measure low pH's like 4.0

A lidded jar that can hold 3 cups

Unsulfured molasses

Non-chlorinated water (or chlorinated tap water that has been left to stand for a day)

1. Sterilize the jar by washing it and immersing it in boiling water. Cool and add 2½ cups of warm or room temperature non-chlorinated water

2. Add 2 Tbs of unsulfured molasses

3. Add 2Tbs of EM-1 (Effective Microorganisms)

4. Add ½ tsp of ceramic powder (optional)

5. Stir Well

6. Cover the jar with the lid (anaerobic process) and keep in a warm place.

The warmer the jar location, the faster the organisms multiply. After about a week, test the brew with pH paper every few days. When the pH drops to 4.0, the brew called Activated EM is ready.

The ceramic powder in both the Activated EM and the bokashi is an optional ingredient. It is a helpful ingredient down, but not completely necessary. It can generally be found online from the same vendors that supply the EM microorganisms.

Activating the Effective Microorganisms

Sterilize a jar

Add 2 ¹/₂ cups of non-chlorinated water

Add 2 Tbs of molasses

Add 2 Tbs of EM-1

Optional ¹/₂ tsp of ceramic powder

Stir well

Cover and allow fermentation to pH of 4.0 or lower

A strip of pH paper that can measure 4.0 or lower pH

Test the pH of the Activated EM

Directions for Making the Bokashi Compost Accelerant

You will need:

Activated EM (make sure it is pH 4.0 or less)

Ceramic Powder (optional)

Sea Salt (optional)

Wheat or Rice Bran (Wheat is cheaper – and larger quantities of rice or wheat bran can be found at farm supply or animal feed stores.)

Unsulfured Molasses

Non-chlorinated water

A mixing container that can hold 3½ lbs. of bran (about 14 cups)

A clean plastic bag (at least 5 gallon capacity) with a twist tie

1. Sterilize the mixing container.

2. Add 3½ lbs of bran (14 ¼ cups).

3. Sprinkle in 2 tsp of ceramic powder (optional).

4. Sprinkle in 2 tsp of sea salt (optional).

5. Mix these dry ingredients together.

6. Place 2 cups of non-chlorinated water in a clean container.

7. Add 2 tsp of molasses to the water.

8. Add 2 tsp of Activated EM to the water.

9. Stir and add the water mixture to the bran mixture.

10. Mix well until the bran is consistently moist. Hands work best.

11. Transfer to a clean plastic bag and close with a twist tie.

Keep in a warm place for a week or so.

**Wash container with bleach
Rinse thoroughly**

**Zero the weight of the container
and add 3¹/₂ lbs of bran**

Add optional ceramic powde

Add optional sea salt

Add 2tsp molasses to 2 cups water

Add 2 tsp of your Activated EM

Stir well

Add liquids to bran mixture

Mix until evenly moist

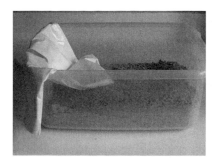

Place in clean bag or other air tight container

Ferment a week or two

When cold, ferment near a low wattage lightbulb

Bokashi may take anywhere from 3 days (in an ambient temperature of 97 degrees F) to over 2 weeks (72 to 80 degree range.) When the bokashi is done it should have a clean, sweet and sour smell.

If making activated EM or bokashi in colder weather you can keep the batches warm by placing the jar of activated EM or plastic bag of bokashi in a box or basket with a 15 watt (or lower wattage) light bulb to raise the temperature. Make sure the lightbulb won't become too hot or come into contact with a material that can catch fire easily.

If your batch smells bad rather than having a clean sweet/sour yeasty smell, it means that something went wrong and the batch should be discarded. Fuzzy or foul smelling molds are also signs that the batch is defective. It is all right to see some fungal mycelium—these look whitish and threadlike—but fuzzy molds should be removed. To avoid these problems, measure well (if the batch is too wet, problems may develop) and make sure all containers and utensils are clean and not harboring unwanted microorganisms.

Whitish growths are okay

It may take quite a few months to get through this sized batch of bokashi and the bokashi may start to get moldy before you can finish using the batch. To avoid this, its good to cooperate with one or two other home gardeners and split up the batches and the batch making. Or you can spread out a newly finished batch of bokashi on a tarp or plastic sheeting and sun dry it. The organisms will become active when mixed with moist kitchen scraps. However, the dried out bokashi does seem to be less effective in eliminating odors. Sprinkle a bit of bokashi into your kitchen compost bucket every day or two.

Bokashi drying on plastic sheet

Composting in Your Kitchen

The best part of bokashi composting is the speed with which you'll be able to bury the nourishing material in your garden. The speed does vary a bit because of temperature variations through the year. In warm seasons it's not uncommon to cycle a five gallon bucket of compost every month. Composting is a beneficial recycling and sustainability enterprise, so go ahead and feel virtuous if you really start bokashi-ing. The other great benefits are the low cost and space-saving efficiency of this do-it-yourself compost.

What to Put in the Bokashi Bucket

Only use plant material in your compost. Eggshells, and meat scraps are more susceptible to the investigations of backyard wild life, and that could prove messy. I once noticed maggots squirming in the compost bucket, presumably laid there by the mother fly attracted to the eggshells sitting on top. Since I collect my own seeds for starting the next year's crops I also don't put in random seeds from store bought vegetables (peppers in particular). Peelings, cores, stems, roots, leaves, coffee grounds from the kitchen counter all go into the compost bucket, also, all the inedible parts of the crops themselves. After the first frost there is usually a great deal of plant material to dispose of in your vegetable patch and around the yard. It can all be composted. When there's too much material for your available buckets, you can use white plastic garbage bags as an expedient replacement. Add bokashi to these simple bags, allow a few weeks for the material to break down a bit and bury the contents before the ground freezes. By the time spring planting comes around, the buried material will be fully broken down and the soil ready to be planted.

How to Use the Compost

As mentioned before, it's best to have at least two buckets for the job— one for collecting new scraps and the other holding contents that are further along in decomposition. Well fitting lids are essential for keeping out pets and vermin. (It is not harmful to pets, but you might not want to share it with them.) The bokashi organisms don't require air and closed buckets will contain odors.

If you don't want to be exposed to odors at all, you might want buckets (particularly the further along bucket) with spigots on the bottom to drain any liquids that accumulate. The liquid will be loaded with friendly microbes and can be beneficially poured down drains to help keep them clean, or poured on top of the garden soil. It's possible to buy buckets that are already tapped with spigots — a more expensive proposition — and it's also possible to buy a spigot and install it yourself. Check beer making supply stores or online sources for inexpensive plastic spigots. If you already own a drill and the proper sized drill bit, you should be able to purchase and tap a five gallon bokashi bucket for under ten dollars.

How to Tap a Plastic Bucket with a Spigot

Mark the location of the spigot on the bucket

Drill hole with a drill bit that is $^1/_8$ inch larger than the spigot

Ready for insertion of the spigot

Insert the spigot

Caulk if necessary

Ready to be filled

It's also possible to forego draining of the compost, however, this does create more odor. As I mentioned previously, I use a smaller bucket for indoor collection that fills in about a week or two. It's sprinkled with bokashi every day or so as it fills with waste. I keep it in the kitchen until full and it stays relatively odor free. Then I pour that amount into my outside bucket that is twice the size. I admit, that pail can be smelly when the lid is lifted up, so perhaps a spigot on the outside bucket will be worth it to some people. But I do recommend using a smaller bucket indoors and a larger size bucket outdoors because it works out well for burying the compost. One bucket is filling in the kitchen, two smaller bucketfuls are fermenting outside, and by the time the third kitchen bucket is full, the composted material is usually ready to be emptied from the outdoor bucket and buried in the garden. For me, this cycle takes about four to five weeks.

When you think of compost, and perhaps in the past you've bought bags of it from a garden center, you may have a mental picture of it as a dark, loose, lightweight dirt. Bokashi compost does not look at all like this. It more resembles exactly what it is -- rotting plant material. It's not very pretty, but you won't have to look at it long because you'll be burying it underneath the surface of the soil.

There may be times when your garden is so well stocked with crops that you may not be able to bury any bokashi. And you certainly can't bury it in winter when the ground is frozen. At times like these, you may have to invest in a third compost bucket or plastic trash bags to store the compost until space opens up in your vegetable patch. In this year-round system of multiple cropping, where crops are finishing while others will soon be planted, there's usually not too long a wait to bury the accumulated bokashi compost. Once the compost is buried underground, the decomposition process speeds up considerably, especially in warm weather. Generally, though, delay the planting of seeds or seedlings in the composted area for about two weeks.

If your fall garden clean up yields multiple plastic bags of decomposing compost, these bags can be placed over root crops like beets, carrots, parsnips, potatoes to keep the ground they're growing in warmer, so you can harvest them later. If you wish to collect the seeds of these

Burying the Bokashi Compost

Dig a trench 4 to 5 inches deep

Add an inch to two inch layer of bokashi compost

Turn bokashi under, a shovelful at a time

Buried compost

biennial root crops, these compost bag coverings can sometimes keep the plants alive through the winter and thus able to flower and make seeds the following spring. Tree leaves that have been raked up around the yard may also be composted in plastic bags as well.

Once finished crops have been cleared away and space for more compost is available, dig a shovel wide trench at a depth of four or five inches. Add an inch or two of compost then insert the shovel into the soil below the composted material and turn it over so the compost is buried even deeper. In digging this first trench you'll usually have to pile the dirt you removed in the first trench into the next area to be dug. There's no getting around this because usually with overlapping cropping, you'll be burying in areas that are close to growing plants. In your next trench, place the accumulated dirt onto the first trenched area and repeat the burying steps. Fill the final trench by evening out all the soil in the newly composted area with your shovel or a garden hoe.

Compost Tea

Another way to provide plentiful and quick nutrition to soil and plants is to apply microorganism-rich compost tea to both the soil around plants and directly on plants as a foliar spray. Compost tea is very easy to make at home. It can be ready for use in about two days and can be applied as frequently as you like. Plants fed a lot of compost tea grow large and healthy and resist pests and diseases more effectively.

This method of growing microorganisms differs from the EM method because it is an aerobic process and relies on other kinds of beneficial, naturally occuring microorganisms. Since these are aerobic (using oxygen) life forms, their reproduction can be sped up by providing an oxygen rich environment through piping air to the brew ingredients.

Since, in making this tea, we're growing bacteria and other organisms, I recommend keeping the process as safe as possible by using only plant sourced and not animal sourced ingredients. However, these cautionary words are not meant to be discouraging words. Applying any kind of compost is applying microorganisms, whether we've bought a bag of compost at the nursery or brewed it ourselves. Microorganisms are essential to plant growth.

If you are planning to make the compost tea and have only chlorinated city water at your disposal, then allow several buckets of tap water to stand for at least 24 hours to dissipate the chlorine gas. The chlorine will not allow microorganisms to grow. You will need unchlorinated

Grow big healthy plants with bokashi composting and compost tea

water for both the brewing process and for diluting the compost tea when applying it to plants.

How to Make Compost Tea

You will need:

One five gallon bucket

Four gallons of unchlorinated water

One small aquarium bubbler with tubing, air stone, and a weight

2 cups of compost in a porous cloth (cut off panty hose works well)

2 Tbs of unsulphured molasses

2 Tbs of fertilizer - kelp or other plant based liquid is preferred

2 Tbs of rock dust, such as azomite or humic shale (optional)

Aquarium bubbler, plastic tubing and air stone

Once all the ingredients are gathered, it will take only a few minutes to set up the brewing process. Disinfect and rinse the bucket. Set the weighted airstone into the bottom of the bucket. (Since I've done some interesting preliminary research on crystal energy and its potential enhancement of life processes, I use a quartz crystal to weight the airline.) Add the other ingredients. Plug in the bubbler and aerate the brew for twenty-four to thirty hours or so.

Pour a little bleach into a five gallon bucket

Wipe bleach across all inside surfaces

Rinse well and fill with four gallons of water . Allow tap water to sit for twenty-four hours

Making compost tea is a good use for rainwater, if available

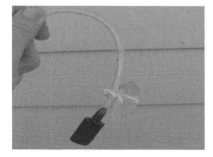

Attach a weight to the tubing or the airstone. Here I'm using a quartz crystal to add subtle energies

Place the weighted tubing into the bucket and plug in the bubbler.

Use an all plant-based source for the compost microorganisms

Add about two cups of compost to a porous cloth, such as cut off pantyhose or cheesecloth

Place the compost "teabag" in the bubbling water. It will eventually submerge.

Add two tablespoons of molasses

Add two tablespoons of liquid kelp, or other liquid fertilizer and/or rock dusts

Allow the mixture to brew for twenty-four to thirty hours as microorganisms multiply

Applying the Compost Tea

When applying compost tea to the soil, dilute the tea in the ratio of two parts water to one part compost tea. Plants can also absorb nutrients through their leaves, and compost tea makes an excellent foliar spray. Make the foliar spray solution more concentrated in a ratio of one part water to two parts compost tea. An ordinary spray bottle works fine, but may quickly tire your hand. A pressurized spray bottle is well worth the expense, if you decide to try the foliar spray method.

Fill one third of the watering can with compost tea

Fill the rest with non-chlorinated water

A pressurized spray bottle will spare your hands some muscle fatigue.

3

Higher

When ground space is at a premium, building upwards is the age-old solution, and this strategy holds for the vegetable garden, as well. To maximize the square footage you can devote to crops, you'll have to add height to the garden by increasing the number of plants you stake to grow vertically. This chapter shows how to build simple, reusable, reconfigurable plant towers and supports from supplies you can easily purchase from building and plumbing supply stores. PVC plumbing pipes and the plastic fixtures that connect them make excellent building materials that can not only be assembled quickly (without the need for nails and screws) these structures can also be disassembled for winter storage, if desired.

What kind of plants can grow vertically to conserve space?

Tomatoes will naturally scramble on the ground, but they don't have any problem being trained to grow upward. A six foot tomato plant can provide scores of tomatoes in the course of a summer.

Five tomato plants can produce a multitude of tomatoes in a three by five foot area

Plant five of them in a three by four foot area (stick to the same variety if you want to collect their seeds for next season) and you'll have plenty of tomatoes to eat fresh and some to can as well.

Peas should be grown on vertical trellises. In small spaces, the biggest food yield will come from growing the edible-podded snow peas or sugar snap peas. Actually peas are wonderful to grow because they can be sown directly in the ground in late winter in most climates. The pea harvest will then be finished by early summer and the same structure can be used to support winter squash vines or melons, which will just be needing support when the pea vines are finishing up.

Green beans come in both bush and climbing varieties. Beans are warmth-loving crops that can only be planted after the last frost date. Unless you live in a very warm climate, you're not likely to harvest more than one crop of beans in a year. If your warm weather lasts well into October, then climbing varieties may serve you well. A summer bean crop growing on a dual season trellis could be preceded by a crop of early finishing spring greens like spinach or lettuce. In the next chapter, I'll show how to start beans in the greenhouse and use its wall and roof supports for a summer bean trellis.

If fall frosts come very early in your area, you should probably choose bush bean varieties. The one year I grew climbing beans we had a frost in early September when the bean plants were just starting to produce well. Thereafter, I've only grown bush beans. I space them closely and keep them picked and they continue to produce all summer until the first frost.

Cucumbers are available in climbing varieties as well as bush type varieties. Training cucumber vines upwards saves a lot of space, so I heartily recommend vining types for small space gardeners. My more important recommendation, when it comes to cucumbers, is to seek out burpless varieties that don't turn bitter. I've harvested too many summer crops of bitter, inedible cucumbers, but I've had great results with various burpless varieties that climb vigorously, produce abundantly, and never develop an unpleasant taste.

Winter Squash, Pumpkins, Melons. Unless you want to dedicate most of your vegetable plot to growing winter squashes and pumpkins, you'll have to grow them upward on stable support structures. They put out very long vines with very large leaves and take up a lot of space if left to scramble on the ground. With the raised structure in this book, you can grow six winter squash plants in a three by four foot space or twelve plants in a three by eight foot space.

Site Concerns

One of the most challenging parts of the garden planning is keeping in mind all the various factors that go into choosing where to plant a particular vegetable. In chapter four, I provide plans to most effectively multicrop through a year in order to rotate plants so they're not taking out the exact same sets of nutrients from the same square inches of soil, or building up the conditions their pests enjoy year after year. Having these tall structures in the garden does complicate the plan because they can't be sited where they will shade other plants too much. If the long sides of your garden are the north and south sides, then place the tall plants on the northern side to receive the sunshine from the south. However, if the long sides of your garden are the east and west sides,

peas on strings hung from
a dual season tower

climbing cucumber vines

**Shorter plants in the south
Taller plants in the north**

then place the tall plants on the eastern side to receive the more ample afternoon light from the west. These are generalized suggestions, but your own local shade conditions from buildings and trees may make this general advice unfeasible for your particular space.

Building with PVC Pipes

Admittedly, pvc pipes and pipe connectors may seem a bit out of place in the vegetable garden, but they have so many advantages as a building material for plant supports. They are easy to cut, durable and sturdy, yet lightweight and portable. They come in standard sizes, as do the connector parts that can join them together into many different configurations. Plant supports made from these materials can be easily snapped together for summer duty or taken apart for winter storage. They are also an inexpensive investment that will last for years.

If you were the type of child who enjoyed constructing things from building block toys or lego blocks, then the activity of putting together pvc structures may bring back fond memories. Tinker toys were a popular amusement when I was growing up, and using these commonly found plumbing parts was pretty close to my childhood experience with tinker toys — kind of fun.

¾ inch pipe cutter

Four years into it, I'm still using the same pipes and connectors I started with. I recommend using ¾ inch pvc pipes and connectors. They are incredibly strong and durable for this purpose. To cut these pipes a ¾ inch pipe cutter comes in handy, but a saw can also be used. It doesn't take very long to cut through the plastic pipe. Armed with a tape measure, a pipe cutter, a hammer, a block of wood (to blunt the impact of hammer strikes on the connectors) and a shovel, you can put together and set all the trellises you'll find in this chapter as well as the put together/take apart greenhouse you'll find in the next.

Commonly found pipe connectors

Since I reuse the pipes for making the different structures, I cut the pipes into standard lengths that minimize waste, somewhat like a modular system. The pipes are sold in ten foot lengths, and cutting these in half into five foot lengths works well. Another standard length I use is sixteen inches. Fifteen inches is even more efficient, but I like a

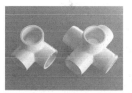

harder to find pipe connectors

slightly larger greenhouse and 16 inches is simply larger than 15. There will be some expense for the pipes and fittings, but they can be reconfigured to use in the greenhouse you build in the fall.

Many people will not be able to transport ten foot pvc pipes from the store to their homes, so shopping at a store that will cut pipes in half may be necessary. The other supply you'll need is twine or string for training the vining plants up these structures. Plants will not grip the slippery pipe surfaces, so twine or string is essential.

Tomato Supports

Tomato plants have a naturally vining nature and the growing branches can be encouraged to spiral around vertical supports. The tall and vey simple and strong tomato supports shown here take advantage of this typical behavior of the tomato plant.

Three upright posts connected at the top and buried four inches into the soil are strong enough to support a six foot tomato plant of a full indeterminate variety. The open design alllows access to all parts of the plants.

How to Build the Tomato Tower

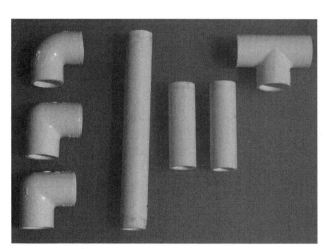

Gather three 90° elbow connectors and one T.
Cut ¾ in. pvc pipe into one 8 inch length
and two 3 ½ inch lengths

Cut three pipe lengths of five feet or more

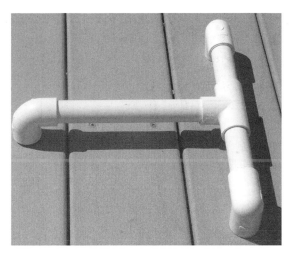

**Insert the two shorter pipe lengths into both sides of the T and the longer length into the end of the T
Place elbows on all three ends**

Set up with three initial lengths of twine

Create the top connecting piece as shown above. The five or six foot lengths of pvc pipe (the legs) are inserted into the bottom ends of the elbow connectors. The structure is then ready to be settled in the soil. Set the pipes to a depth of about four inches or so.

The three horizontal bars at the top will hold the twine lengths that tomato branches can be guided around — in spiral fashion. This way, the branches help to hold themselves up. Twine can be tied to a top bar with the other end loosely tied to the base of a branch that needs support. Or instead of tying the bottom end to a tomato branch, the twine can be staked to the soil with a small metal stake. Begin early on with the leading tomato branch by guiding it around and around a length of twine. Drop other lines to guide other branches up as needed over the following weeks, or set up the tower with three strings in place to be used when needed as shown above.

Twine can be staked into the soil

The Constrictor Knot for Tying Twine to the Bars

(Any knot will do but this is a good one.)

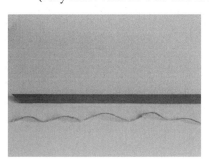
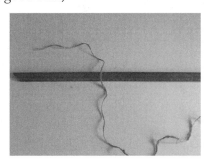
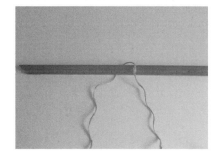

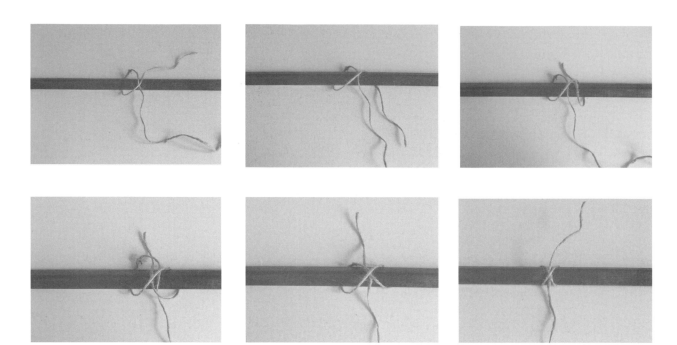

The constrictor knot is very useful for attaching the twine to the top bars. It is not necessary to use this kind of hitch, but it is very neat and doesn't loosen easily. Once in place, it can be wound around the bar to keep the line taut.

Five Tomato Plants in a 4 x 3 foot Area

Easily accomodates 6 foot tall tomato plants

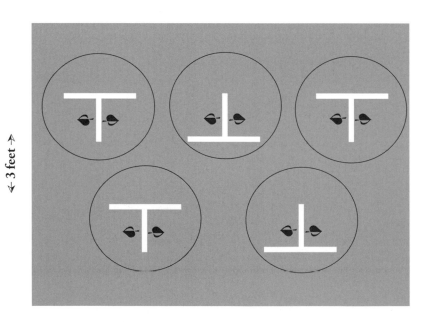

← 3 feet →

← 4 feet →

A lot of people prune tomato plants, but I don't think it's necessary. All the extra green growth makes for a greater sugar factory for the plant. I find temperature — either too hot or too cold to be the greater inhibitor of fruit production.

Store flat for winter or reuse parts to construct a greenhouse

How to Make the Cucumber Trellis

This trellis has only a 1¹/₂ x 2 foot base area, yet six cucumber plants can be grown underneath.

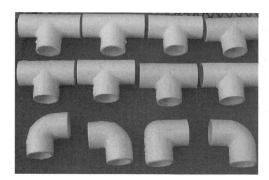

Gather together eight T connectors
and four 90° elbows

Cut four five foot pipe lengths,
four 15 or 16 inch pipe lengths,
four 5 inch pipe lengths,
and six 3 inch pipe lengths

3. Insert two 5 ft. poles
into the ends of two Ts.
Two 5 in pipes (stakes) are
inserted into the base ends
of the Ts. Join the poles
with a 15 or 16 in crossbar

4. Make a second frame

Place T connectors on each end
of the remaining 15 or 16 in pipes

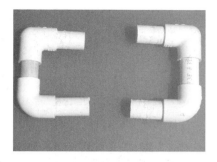

Insert the six 3 in. pipes into the
four elbow connectors

Insert the corner assemblies into the Ts at the
ends of the 15 or 16 in pipes

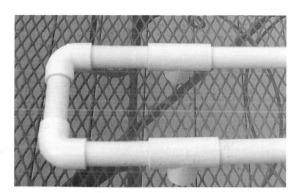

Push togeher firmly

The completed top assembly

Insert the front and back frames
into the top assembly.
Spread the frames apart
by angling the top assembly
down on one side

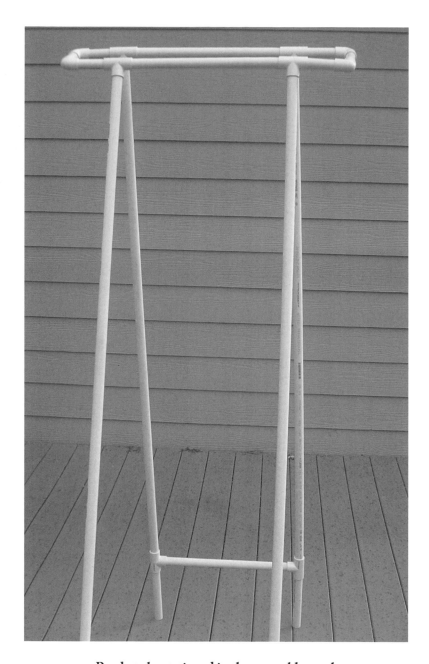

Ready to be stationed in the vegetable patch

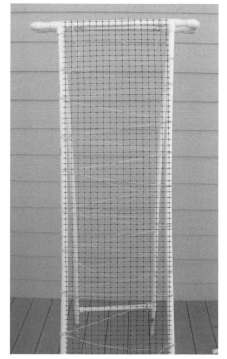

Covered with Trelis Netting

Once the cucumber trellis has been assembled, it can be sited in the garden where cucumbers are to be grown. Bury the bottom stakes four or so inches deep for stability. The cucumber vines will need twine or trellis netting to climb upon. Trellis netting can be attached to the frames. Twine can be strung between the top assembly and bottom crossbars or a network of twine can be criss crossed side to side around the pipes to provide horizontal support.

Stringing the Frames Side to Side

Tightly wrap pipes from side to side going up at an angle

Wrap string around the pipe

Under the string

Around the pipe again

Back to the other side, and around that pipe

Under the string. Arond the pipe and back to the other side.

This inexpensive and quick set up has worked very well for me. If the string is wound tightly, the weight of the cucumber fruits does not drag the strings out of position on the poles.

A more permanent string placement can be attained by drilling holes through the pipes and lacing the string through the holes from side to side. You will need an electric drill and drill bit at least $3/8$ th of an inch so the holes you will thread through are nice and roomy. As with the stringing technique above, stagger the holes from side to side so that the string will angle upwards as you thread from one side to the other.

Drill hole closer to the top on one pole

Drill hole further from the top on the opposite pole

Wrap string with sturdy tape.

Thread through the drill holes from side to side

Dual Season Grow Tower

The next structure has the strength and stability needed for growing squash or melon vines with their heavy hanging fruits. One Long Island cheese squash I grew weighed in at 10 lbs 7ozs and was easily supported by the tower I'd constructed. In my latest growing season, a 3 x 7 foot tower supported twenty-two good sized butternut squashes. The structure can be made smaller or larger depending on the garden area you wish to devote to large vining plants. Extra height and anchoring parts are added to the structure for convenient placing of twine for pea vines. Since peas can be planted in late winter and squashes grow in summer, two crops can be grown in more or less the same footprint.

Ladder-like uprights support a high horizontal tier
Use four ladder uprights for a 3 x 4 foot area or six ladders, as shown here, for a 3 x 8 foot growing area

Though strong enough for heavy fruits, children should be discouraged from climbing on this structure.

For a Six Ladder Tower You Will Need:

28 — T connectors

8 — 90° elbow connectors

36 — 20 inch pipe lengths for uprights - use ³/₄ inch pvc pipe

16 — 15 or 16 inch pipe lengths for crossbars and pea vine extensions

4 — 32 inch pipe lengths for top tier horizontals

2 — 7 foot pipe lengths for the long top tier horizontals

Optional — 10 additional T connectors to anchor twine for pea vines

Attach T connectors to the ends of the 20 inch uprights   **Connect with a 15 or 16 inch crossbar**   **Tap together gently with a hammer**

Add more uprights and crossbars, tapping each into place

Build to about five feet high
Attach 90° elbow connectors to the top ends of the uprights

Two pairs of ladder-like side supports ready to be connected together

Two end ladders with 15 inch extensions on top for stringing pea vines. Use Ts (not elbows) to connect these extensions at the top

Connect two pairs of ladders with 32 inch pipe lengths

Imprint the ground where the structure will be settled Move the structures aside temporarily to work on deepening these holes

**Drill the holes in the soil
by hammering on a section of
broomstick or dowel**

Set one end ladder in the ground

Insert the 7 foot pipe lengths into the T connectors in the end ladder

64

Set the second end ladder on the other side and
insert the 7 foot pipe lengths into those T connectors

Tie the crossbers and long bars together with cable ties

. . . or twine

T connectors on the end ladders anchor the top strings of the pea vine trellis

T connectors with short pipe lengths are good for anchoring strings at ground level

Anchor the stakes in the ground

Tie strings from one stake through the middle stake to the stake at the other end

Tie strings or twine from end to end

Wrap twine over a top string, under the ground level string and again over the top string about three or so inches beyond the prior string position

The middle stake holds the string closer to ground level

For a smaller tower to cover a 3 x 4 foot area, you will need a total of four ladder-like supports — two pairs set opposite one another to make a square arrangement.

Pea or bean seeds can be planted on both sides of both nets. Strung like a harp, plants will find their way up this trellis without any further help. Twine or string can be re-used a second year if unwound carefully at the end of the harvest. For manageability, wrap the twine around a stick as you unwind it. Ready-made trellis netting will set up more quickly, but make sure your hands can slip through the netting to harvest the pea pods.

**Wrap twine around a stick when unstringing the trellis
if you want to re-use the twine another year**

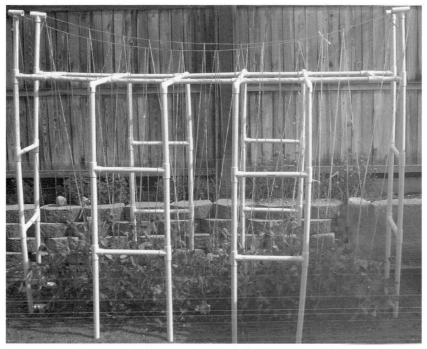

Plant peas in late winter to harvest in late spring

Plant melons or squash outside the perimeter of the pea vines

The squash vines will not grip the pvc pipe surfaces. It will be necessary to tie vines with twine or string up the supports until they reach the upper crossbars where they can drape themselves horizontally. You will most likely have to keep an eye on the vines for a while.

This dual purpose tower helps to maximize space since two crops can be grown in the tower area during overlapping seasons. In the next chapter we'll get into other ways to grow multiple crops a year.

All of the tall structures in this chapter can help support shade canopies during the summer doldrums. In setting out these tall garden structures and the greenhouse, you might give some thought to placement for later draping of burlap or shade cloth over the garden for a few weeks.

4

Longer

Strategies for Extending the Growing Season

Extension of the garden season through continuous cropping will consistently bring greater food yields to your gardening efforts. If you decide to build the greenhouse that I show in this chapter, it is possible to harvest fresh food from the garden ten months a year or more, depending on your climate zone.

Success with this system depends on knowing which vegetables to plant when. Some vegetables require warm weather, some cool weather, which is lucky for us, since we can take advantage of the differences to extend the growing season. The information in this book is a general guide to crop planting by season. More specific dates for particular locations can generally be found at state agricultural extension websites. Local gardening stores and local news sites may also have good information about what to plant when in your area. In January 2012 the USDA published new climate zone guidelines that changed the climate zone map. Now plants that need warmer temperatures can be grown in more northern locales or planting times can be moved up a bit.

Cool Weather Crops

Sow In Late Winter to Early Spring
And/Or Mid- Summer for Fall Harvest

Arugula	Broccoli	Brussels Sprouts	Cabbage
Cauliflower	Kale	Kohrabi	Lettuce
Mesclun Mix	Onions	Spinach	Turnip

And peas of all varieties. It's not likely to get more than one crop of peas in a year. If you try to grow a fall crop, there may not be enough insects around to pollinate the pea flowers if they bloom.

Crops That Can Survive a Light Frost
Sow Directly in Early to Mid-Spring

Beet	Carrot	Fennel	Parsnip
Potato	Swiss Chard		

Warm Weather Crops
Sow After All Danger of Frost Is Over

Bean	Cucumber	Eggplant	Melon
Okra	Pepper	Pumpkin	Summer squash
Tomato	Winter Squash	Zucchini	

Many of these warm weather crops can be started early indoors on sunny windowsills or with artificial lighting. If you wish to grow eggplant, pepper, and tomato from seed you will almost certainly need to start them indoors or in a greenhouse to be sure that you can harvest their fruits in colder climate zones. In the greenhouse, you can start them in seed pots about eight weeks before the last frost date. Or you can seed them directly in the greenhouse soil at this time for later transplanting when the weather is a warmer.

You will have to look after these tender little seedlings in the greenhouse. Early in spring, they may succumb to plunging nighttime temperatures, so if extreme cold is predicted, bring the seedlings indoors over night. In later spring, snails and slugs may wander into the greenhouse to feast on these tender seedlings. For these reasons, it's best to move the pots of eggplant, pepper, and tomato seedlings into hanging baskets that you can easily move into the house, when temperatures drop precipitously, or suspend from the greenhouse ridge pole once the gastropods have emerged. More information about greenhouse planting will be found later in this chapter.

A wire basket can hold several small plastic or peat pots

Warming Up Spring Chills

Water is one of the few substances that we encounter in its three phases of gas, liquid, and solid on a daily basis. On a hot day with a lot of humidity (gaseous water in the air) we can go to the kitchen and get ourselves a glass of water with ice — just like that! We're literally surrounded by water. Even desert regions have moisture in the air and at night, when temperatures drop, desert humidities can reach 100 percent and condense out as dew on rocks and other surfaces.

When water molecules change from gas to liquid and from liquid to ice, energy in the form of heat calories is either released or absorbed. Do you want to know how to keep something cold at a picnic without using ice? Wrap it in cloth or newspaper soaked with water and place it in a sunny spot. As the liquid water molecules evaporate into the gaseous phase, energy in the form of heat is absorbed by the water vapor leaving the cloth or newspaper with less energy — fewer calories of heat. This is also the reason why humans sweat. The surface of our bodies lose heat as the water in the sweat evaporates, thus we cool off.

Freezing does the opposite — releasing heat energy into the surrounding atmosphere. These phase changes and the energy exchanges that occur can be used to great advantage by the knowledgeable gardener to help mitigate the effects of both low and high temperatures.

I once read a theory about the purpose of the chinampas found around the archaeological sites of Mexico. Chinampas were the raised rectangular growing fields surrounded by water that were built by the indigenous Mexicans. Anthropologists had long speculated about the purpose of this agricultural arrangement. The theory I read postulated that the water surrounding the fields allowed the people to start their crops earlier, given the temperature modulating effects of water phase changes. Water freezing in the surrounding canals added enough heat to the chinampas for plants to survive in early spring. The home gardener can also use these same principles of physics to help warm up plants in cold weather and help cool them in hot temperatures.

Mini Chinampas with Recycled Bottles

Like the Aztecs, we can experiment with starting our crops early, especially if we have spare seeds to try again if our early starts fail. Vessels holding water can be circled around frost tender plants to help them withstand the frosty nights. Most of us regularly dispose of empty bottles and cartons, but here we can view them as a valuable resource.

No matter what time of year you are reading this book, you might want to start saving containers that you previously have sent to the recycle bin. Taller containers are better than shorter containers, plastic or waterproofed cardboard are better than glass. Water expands when it freezes, and glass bottles can break from the pressure of the expanding ice inside. It usually takes at least five containers to tightly surround a seedling, so you will need to save plenty of vessels. My preference is for half-gallon plastic milk containers. They are sturdy and tall enough to get a tomato seedling though spring until the danger of frost is gone.

After planting the seedling in the ground, surround the plant with containers filled two thirds to three quarters full of water. You have to leave room at the top for the expansion of ice. Make sure there are no gaps between bottles. Once the arrangement is set, mound soil outside the base of the containers to hold them upright and in place. On warm spring days, water in the containers may evaporate, so containers may have to be refilled over the course of their use.

To further protect the tender plants from cold weather, cover them with the kind of garden cloth that lets in air and moisture and keep them covered all spring until all danger of frost is gone. Or keep a watchful eye on daytime and especially nighttime temperatures and cover the plants with any kind of cloth or plastic sheeting until temperatures warm up again. Mound soil on top of the cloth to seal all possible entryways to the seedlings if you wish to keep out slugs or snails.

If you have enough bottles collected, you can set out eggplant, peppers and tomatoes three weeks to one month in advance of the first frost when surrounded by these bottles of water. This method would probably also work with cucumbers and squashes, but I have not experimented with these varieties. I think it should work if you sow the seeds about three weeks before your last frost date and not try to start the squashes too early. If you wish to start all these varieties early, start saving bottles. You will need a lot of them.

Plant seedling and surround with bottles three quarters full of water

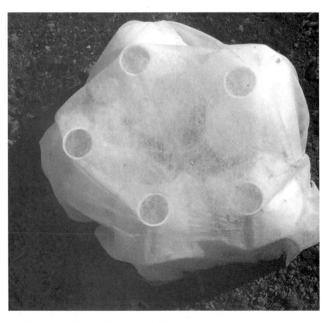

Cover with garden cloth for warmth and protection

Overwintering with Water Warming

Certain plants that are perennial in warmer climates may make it through winter using this strategy. Last year I surrounded a rosemary plant with various containers and covered it with a heavier variety of garden cloth before winter. The plant survived the winter successfully. If there are certain plants you'd like to overwinter for seed collecting the following spring, try surrounding them with water bottles and a sturdy but porous cloth cover.

Vessels of water helped a rosemary plant survive through the winter

How to Make the Flowerpot Cooler

Here's an interesting idea for keeping food frosty without ice or electricity – another practical demonstration of the properties of water that may come in handy some day. Nested, unglazed ceramic pots with wet sand in between allow water to slowly evaporate and cool the inner cavity which can be filled with food.

Tape the hole of a large unglazed ceramic pot

Tape the hole of a smaller pot nested inside

Block the top of the inner pot so it won't fill with sand

Fill the area between the pots with sand

Wet the sand with water

Cover with a wet cloth

Cooling During the High Heat Weeks

A funny thing can happen to tomatoes in the dog days of summer. They get too hot and stop producing fruits. One of the advantages of

Bowls or basins of water in the central square have a cooling effect

the center square plan is that large basins of water can be placed in the central square areas to create a mini-microclimate near the surrounding plants. The evaporating water molecules absorb heat energy and cool the surrounding areas.

Growing plants vertically with high supports has the added advantage that shade cloth or burlap can be partly held up on the tops of these towers. Shade cloth comes in various weights. Thirty percent shade is good for plants. Too much shade of course will cut off too much light. The combination of shade and water basins should help to cool off the garden plants and keep them productive at the height of summer.

A Simple Shade Cloth Canopy

Cut pvc pipes for the corners of the area you wish to cover with shade cloth. Place 3 way Y connectors at the top of each corner post. Connect with pvc pipe crossbars. Attach the shade cloth to the crossbars by wrapping the cloth over the poles and "sewing" short lengths of thin wire through the netting holes where needed.

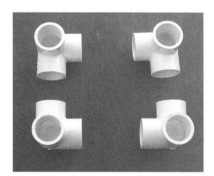

Four 3 way Y connectors

Y's attached to four pipes of at least 5 feet

Connect the corners with crossbars and set the canopy frame in the ground

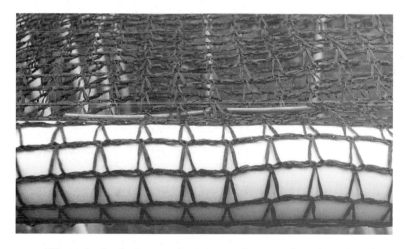

Wrap shade cloth over the pipes and weave short lengths of wire through the perforations like "sewing". Weave in wires where needed on at least two opposite sides of the cloth

Planting The Fall Crop

The other feature of mid-to-late summer is that it's time to plant fall crops. Any crops that are finished or mostly finished, such as winter plants that were grown in the greenhouse, can be fully harvested to make way for new seeds. The beds can be prepared for re-planting. Bokashi can be buried anytime the soil is workable, but allow it to further decay in the ground for at least a week or two before sowing new seeds in that area. The window for sowing fall crops is not a large one. There's not more than two or three weeks to successfully accomplish this from July through early August. With a shade cloth canopy or shade cloth over the greenhouse frame, you may be able to start the fall crop earlier in July.

Good Plants for Fall

Plants that need only about 70 days growth until harvest that can also withstand some frost are good candidates for fall crop planting in most U.S. climates. These varieties include:

Arugula	Beet	Cauliflower	Leaf Lettuce
Kale	Kohlrabi	Mustard	Radish
Spinach	Swiss Chard	Turnip	

Broccoli and cabbage need more time and may be iffier propositions in some climate zones.

The later we push back the harvest in fall the less light there will be for completing the growth cycle. If it's mid August or September and you're just considering a fall crop, it would be better to plan for a greenhouse crop that will be ready for harvest in late winter through spring, depending on what you plant. In the lower light conditions of late fall and winter, plants simply take longer to mature, even if kept warm enough.

When the first frost comes, summer crops will begin to die. Tomatoes, peppers, eggplants, cucumbers, beans, okra, squashes are at the end of their days when frost comes visiting. Keeping an eye on projected nighttime temperatures, it may be possible to cover cold susceptible plants with garden cloth at night and extend their season a little longer. When it's clear that their growing time is unequivocally over, its time to tear out the plants and start composting them. Nothing goes to waste when the plants get turned back into the soil through composting. Make sure there's plenty of bokashi available at this time to add to the containers of plant material. If you run out of plastic buckets, you can use plastic bags to compost the garden waste. Dried up bean stems and tomato stalks are not such desirable pickings for the local wildlife, so there's probably no need to worry that the plastic bags of such stuff will be invaded.

Bags of composting material warm the ground and plant roots beneath

Root crops in the ground at the end of fall can be left in the ground for quite awhile. To extend their harvest even further you can place bags of composting material, even leaf bags, on top of them to keep the soil warmer for longer. The microbial activity in the bags produces some heat to warm the soil beneath. Root crops may even winter over with this treatment, which makes it a lot easier to harvest the seeds of biennial plants. Seed collecting advice will be found in chapter five.

If the fall crops you planted in August are not maturing. You can help them along with extra heat and light. Plants can be covered with garden cloth. Rocks — especially heat retaining lava rocks — can be placed on the central squares of your garden near the fall crops. One of the main reasons for less vigorous growth in fall is the drop off in sunlight. Aluminum foil woven through stakes for support can reflect additional light and warmth on late fall crops.

Aluminum foil reflecting more light on a fall beet crop

A Word About Tomatoes

Each fall, I end up pleasantly surprised by the number of green tomatoes that eventually do ripen. Place them on plates or shallow bowls at room temperature and eat them or refrigerate them as they ripen to red.

Heat retaining lava rock set on the center square

Winter

Building a greenhouse may sound like a daunting prospect, but I've discovered an arrangement that can be put together in a day or so for a cost of about eighty dollars in materials. If you use the pvc pipes from other plant supports, it will cost even less. The pvc pipes that were used for supporting your tomato and cucumber plants can now serve double duty as the walls of the green house. You can use some of the connectors from the tomato and cucumber supports as well, but it will be necessary to buy some additional materials to form the walls and roof of a 6' x 8' greenhouse. The greenhouse crops, even if only planted in December, ensure that food will be ready to eat in the early spring months of March and April. If started even earlier, you may be eating fast growing crops like lettuce and spinach in January or February. With a greenhouse you'll get a good three or four additional months of garden harvesting. The expense of the additional supplies is worth it, especially since the structure will last for many years. The plastic sheeting may have to be replaced every two years or so, depending on conditions. It is possible to repair tears in the plastic with a special clear tape made for plastic sheeting.

The plastic sheeting comes in various weights. I recommend using the 6 mil variety. It is thicker and sturdier, and can stand up to some

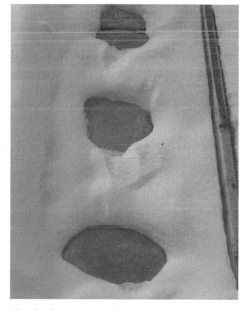

Rocks have melted the snow on the path

snowfall, but only some. I've allowed 5 inches of snow to accumulate on my greenhouse roof before sweeping it off, but I have not tested the actual limits. I think you will probably have to make it a practice to clear the snow off its roof as snow accumulates beyond four or five inches. This temporary greenhouse isn't durable enough to withstand heavy snow loads, nor will it withstand gale force winds without risk of damage or need for adjustment. On ordinary windy days, the greenhouse fares better if it's completely closed up.

Its temporary, portable nature is the biggest virtue of this greenhouse design. It can initially be put together in a day and taken apart in a few minutes for storage. It can be moved around in the garden for general crop rotation, so it's not in the same location year after year (this requires at least two people to lift it up and move it – not because it's heavy, but just to keep the integrity of the connections.) Another option is to remove the plastic sheeting and keep the framing skeleton in place for the following winter. In this case, you might simply rotate the crops within the greenhouse area soil.

When to Erect the Greenhouse

You can start to build the greenhouse anytime your area is ready, but waiting until after you've taken apart the cucumber and tomato supports will save some expense. You won't have to buy as many supplies if you wait until the five foot lengths and connectors are available from the summer plant supports. However, it is best to have composted for the winter's crop in the greenhouse soil before building it — especially if you're burying the compost, as with bokashi. The greenhouse walls may limit your shoveling motions when turning the bokashi deeply under the surface.

The greenhouse absolutely does have to be built before the ground freezes, because you will not be able to sink the pipes in the ground after this point. Also, it's much nicer to build one in cool rather than freezing cold temperatures. It's hard to get a grip on the plastic pipes if your hands are wearing gloves.

If you have to get a late start on planting in the greenhouse, don't worry that you've lost too much time. Sunlight is so diminished in the late fall and early winter that plants don't grow so vigorously even in the greenhouse. Though the plants won't exactly catch up, you'll still have early spring crops to eat even if you've waited until Christmas to plant new seeds. The soil in the greenhouse will have to be watered and a watering can may be a necessary purchase. Stand on the center square and water all around.

How To Build The Greenhouse

You Will Need:

21 — five foot lengths of ³/₄ in. pvc pipe for wall studs

12 — pipe lengths to be measured (about 41 in.) for rafters

18 — sixteen in. pipe lengths

8 — 1¹/₂ in. pipe lengths for turning corners

1 — pipe length to be measured (about 8 feet) for the ridge pole

13 — four way cross connectors

9 — T connectors

6 — 90° elbow connectors

18 — 45° angle connectors

12 — two in. lengths of flexible spa hose or other flexible pipe

The supplies above are for building the frame of the greenhouse. Following are supplies for covering it with a plastic shell.

1 — roll of 25 foot x 10 foot 6 mil plastic sheeting
4 — 28 in lengths of screen wood molding for seam stiffeners
5 — 48 in lengths of screen wood molding for seam stiffeners
32 — clips for holding plastic sheeting to wood seam stiffeners
2 — 7 ½ foot lengths of 2 x 4s for anchoring plastic at ground
2 — 5 ½ foot lengths of 2 x 4s for anchoring plastic at ground

front view of framing

1 ridge pole about 8 feet

6 wall studs on each of the 8 foot sides connect to 6 rafter trusses

5 wall studs form the back wall and 1 ridge pole support extends up from the middle stud

4 wall studs and 1 ridge pole support extends up from a T connector in the center leaving a 3 foot doorway opening in the front wall

side view of framing

Set a 5 ft pipe firmly in the ground starting about 2½ inches in from the corner. Attach a 4 way cross connector at the top. Insert a sixteen inch crossbar firmly into the side slot of the cross connector to find the placement of the next wall stud. Use a hammer and block to firmly set connectors and pipes.

This corner is made with a 90° elbow connector by inserting a 1½ in pipe length into each side of the elbow to connect to the T on the first back wall post

If you obtain a 5 way cross connector, you can make a simpler corner by inserting a 1½ in pipe length into the 5 way and the T

The front and back wall studs are topped with T connectors except at the centers. The back center stud is topped with a cross. The front center joint has an inverted T. These will hold up the ridge pole extenders

Firmly insert 2 inch lengths of ³/₄ inch flexible pipe or tubing into the tops of the cross connectors

The 45° angle connectors on the roof rafter trusses require some play at the point of connection to the wall stud connectors. Spa hose is ideal for stability and flexibility, but other kinds of ³/₄ inch flexible tubing may also work.

Each roof rafter truss is composed of two pipes and three 45° angle connectors. The pipe lengths will be in the neighborhood of 41 inches but may vary depending on whether you've rounded the corners of the walls with elbow connectors or are using 5 way corner connectors. It's best to do some measuring and testing of the lengths

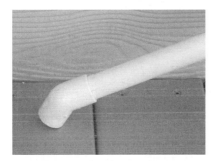 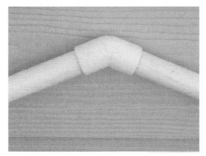 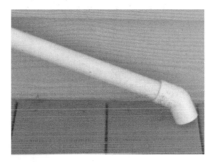

Place and secure the rafters on the flexible hose bits in each wall stud

To determine the height of the ridge pole uprights, insert a length of pipe into a 90° elbow. Then loosely insert a short piece of pipe into the other end of the elbow where the ridge pole will eventually be connected. Place this arrangement under the rafter and mark the length on the upright pipe length. Cut to fit.

Measure and cut the ridge pole. Connect it to the uprights at the front and back ends

Secure the rafter trusses to the ridge pole with cable ties or twine

Framing completed

Covering the Frame with Plastic Sheeting

The plastic sheeting provides a functional covering for the greenhouse that keeps cold exterior air out and sun-warmed interior air in. With the following directions you will be able to cover the greenhouse using one 25 foot by 10 foot roll of 6 mil plastic. There won't be anything to spare, so follow all cutting directions closely. "Seams" connecting plastic sections are made by wrapping the plastic edges to be joined around a thin strip of wood molding then holding the sheeting and wood together with small clamps or clips. Easiest results will be accomplished by clamping the seams more or less together and then correcting and perfecting the seams clamp by clamp. The supplies for covering the greenhouse are listed on page 82.

Below is a front view of the covered greenhouse.

One 25 x 10 ft roll of plastic sheeting

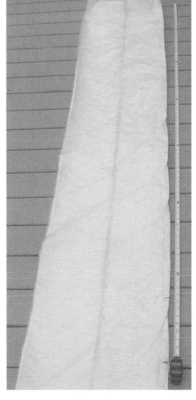

Measure exactly 82 inches from the end of the roll
and cut across all the folds of plastic sheeting.
Reserve this 82 in x 10 ft length for
the front and back sections of the greenhouse.

Drape the bulk of the plastic across one of the
middle supporting rafters. Even the lengths on
both sides

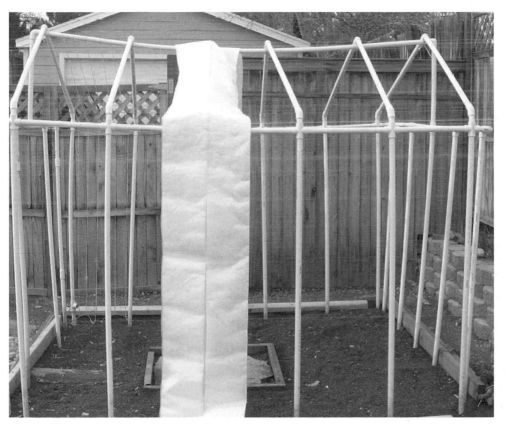

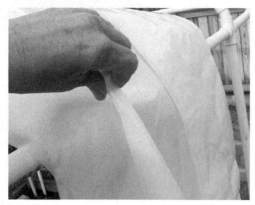

Unfold the sheeting completely to cover the framing on both sides

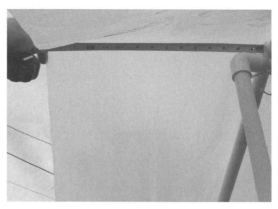

Even out the plastic on the front and back ends of the greenhouse, making sure there is at least twelve inches of overhang on each end.

Attach the plastic sheeting to the 2 x 4 anchoring board on one of the sides by stapling here and there

Roll the 2 x 4 in the plastic sheeting until the wall is somewhat taut.

If you must stand on the soil as you work, use a board to walk on as this will distribute weight more evenly and compress the soil less

Bury the anchoring board with soil for added stability

Repeat these last few steps to anchor the plastic on the other side as well.

Back And Front Walls

Measure and cut the resrve length into two equal pieces of 82 in x 5 ft

Front and back sections of plastic sheeting should be cut to a peak

Mark off 21 inches on
the two sides

Mark the center point at the top

Draw the lines on which to cut

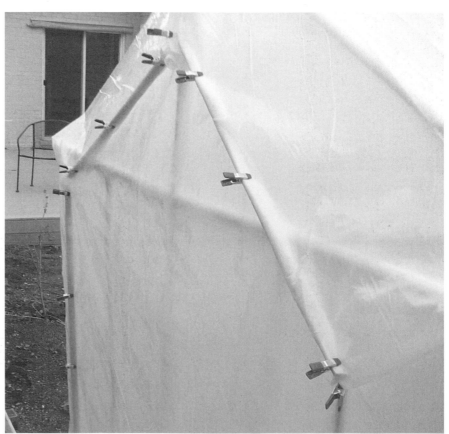

A view of the completed seams
on the back of the greenhouse
to show how they will look
when finished

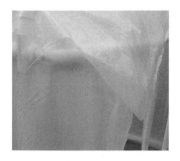

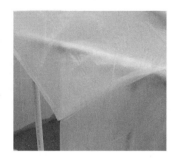

Excess plastic from the sides of the greenhouse should be brought around to the back side with the corners folded at an angle

To construct the back of the greenhouse, gather the four strips of wood screen molding shown below, fourteen or fifteen small clamps, and the back panel of plastic that was cut with a peak.

Two lengths of screen molding cut to 28 in. Two lengths cut to 48 in.

You will need 14 or 15 clamps such as these

These clips have also worked well for me

Even out the back panel. Temporarily clamping it at the top and sides may be helpful

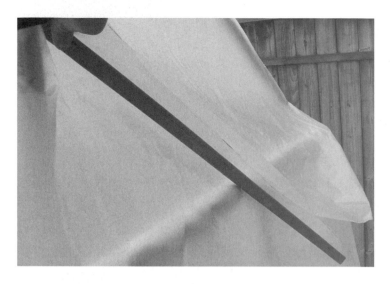

Line up a 28 inch length of screen molding with
the edges of the plastic panels to be joined.
Wrap the plastic downward around the stick
to better shed rain water

First clip

Second clip

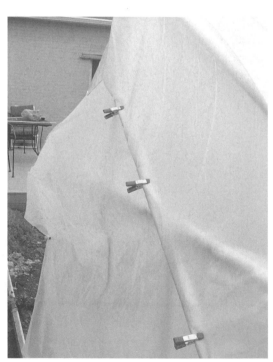

Third clip

Start the seam construction
on the other side of the peak with
the second 28 inch piece of wood

Add a clamp to the center to close any gaps, if needed

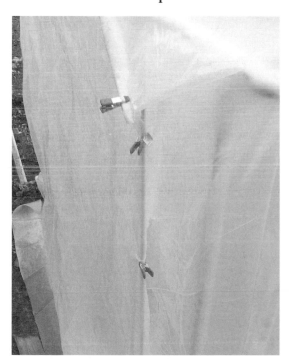

Make a vertical seam on each side with
the 48 inch lengths of wood and
3 or 4 clamps on each side

The back panel attached and clamped

Anchor the bottom by wrapping the plastic around a 2 x 4

The front panel construction begins by repeating the steps used to cut the back panel. However, to create a smoothly opening door flap for entering the greenhouse, the front panel will be constructed in two parts. To do this, mark the sides one and a half inches down from the side edges. Draw a line across and cut.

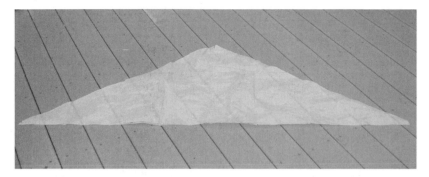

Work with the triangle first. The reserved length will be attached later

Two 28 inch lengths and three
48 inch lengths of screen molding
Gather 16 or so small clamps

Bring excess plastic from the sides
to the front of the greenhouse.
Fold at the corners.
Temporary clamping may be helpful

Construct the seams with the 28 inch
lengths of wood and clamps
using the same techniques
as for the back construction

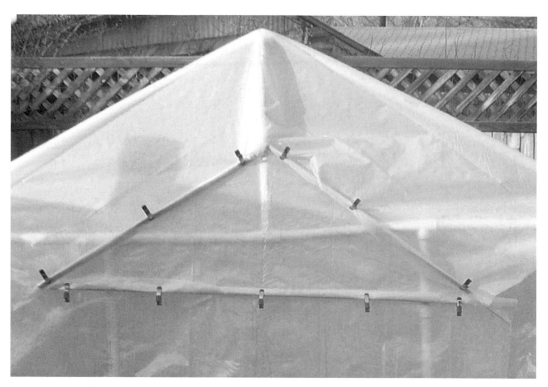

Construct the horizontal seam joining the triangular piece to the reserved piece using a 48 inch length of wood molding.

Construct the side seams using 48 inch lengths of screen molding

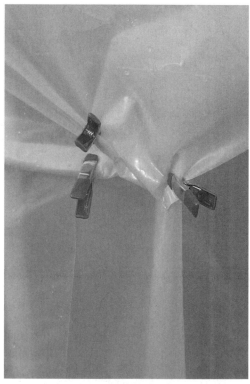

Peak, crossbar, and side seam connected together at the right front corner

Finish constructing the seams on both sides.
Anchor the bottom of the plastic flap by wrapping it around a 2 x 4

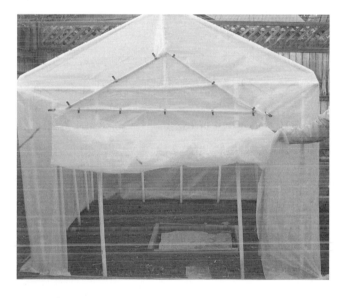

To enter the greenhouse,
undo the bottom two
clips on each side seam to
lift the door flap

The door flap can be
clipped open

The completed greenhouse

Greenhouse Variations

Constructing this greenhouse will allow for a good harvest of cool weather crops in late winter through early spring. In later spring, the greenhouse can be used to start summer seedlings in pots or directly in the greenhouse soil. In summer, if the plastic cover is removed, the greenhouse frame can be used for trellising. Strings can be tied from the ridge pole over the walls and to the ground for climbing vines. Squashes and melons can be tied to the frame and allowed to scramble over the walls and rafters. With shade cloth over the roof, summer seedlings planted for a fall crop can benefit from cooler temperatures.

Tie twine to the frame for a summer bean trellis

Or attach ready-made trellis netting

Drape squash vines over the rafters

Cool temperatures in the greenhouse
with shade cloth or burlap cover

Crops for the Greenhouse

Sow in Fall to Overwinter — or in Winter

Arugula	Beet	Broccoli	Brussels Sprouts
Cabbage	Carrot	Cauliflower	Fennel
Kale	Kohrabi	Lettuce	Mesclun Mix
Spinach	Parsnip	Swiss Chard	Turnip

Root vegetables started in fall or early winter in the greenhouse may decide to flower early in spring instead of making the large bulbous roots we like to eat. I find that waiting to sow until after the winter solstice increases the likelihood for good root development.

Starting Seeds in the Greenhouse

The nightshade family of plants that bear those delicious and extremely popular fruits: tomatoes, eggplants, peppers are usually not harvestable until well into summer. These are often the same plants that succumb to early frosts, as well. To get a good crop of the fruits, you generally have to start the seeds in winter, when the plants couldn't possibly withstand the outdoor temperatures in most locations. Thus, most people buy tomato plants, etc. from nurseries when outdoor temperatures are, at last, suitable. Others start seeds indoors in sunny windows or under grow lights. Starting your own seeds not only saves money, the range of seed varieties available from seed suppliers is generally much wider than nursery or garden center choices of plants. If you want to save money, explore more exotic varieties, or if you've a mind to self-sufficiency and want to start plants from open pollinated seeds you've collected yourself, the greenhouse will be a useful addition to your vegetable garden. Growth indoors or under artificial light can often be anemic and lead to weak, spindly seedlings. Even under plastic, there's so much more light outdoors for plants to make a strong start.

There is some danger of frost inside the greenhouse as well in early spring, especially for the nightshades. Using a dual approach may be the best course. Start pots of seedlings indoors where they can germinate in warmer house temperatures, then introduce them to the greenhouse in mid-to-late spring to enjoy plentiful natural sunlight filtering through the greenhouse roof.

You can plan ahead and leave an area of the greenhouse unplanted to use for later sowing of these frost tender plants. Or you can utilize the center square as your seed pot cultivation space. In the latter case, place your seed starting pots in trays or hanging baskets that can be moved out of the greenhouse in case you yourself need to occupy the center square for weeding, or harvesting, or other maintenance of the greenhouse crops. Then you can move the trays of seedlings back into place on the center square before buttoning up the greenhouse.

To increase the number of plants and minimize the space required to keep them well lit, it can be tempting to start seedlings in very small pots. After many disappointing results using tiny pots, I've come to learn that it's better to start seedlings in pots of at least three inches in diameter or three inches square. The very small pots don't allow enough room for the amount of root expansion the plants need before final planting in the garden soil. You can fit 36 seedling pots on the 2 x 2 foot square center area. Four 15 inch diameter hanging baskets of pots can hang from the ridge pole.

If you are starting those seeds in the greenhouse, you'll want to keep it up and available to keep the seedlings warm until later in spring when you can plant them. Some spring days can be very warm and it's possible that the greenhouse environment will become too hot. Leave two sides of the greenhouse open for cooling airflow at such times, and close up if nighttime temperatures drop into the low forties or below. The frost tender nightshade plants can be planted in the ground about a month or so before your final frost date, if you can surround them with vessels of water and cover them with garden cloth as previously stated in this chapter.

Summer and the Greenhouse

When the weather warms up, and there's no longer a danger of heavy frosts, you can dismantle the greenhouse and store the parts until they are needed for other uses. Harvest all these greenhouse-started plants by July and you can use the same soil area for starting the fall crop of seeds. First compost the soil, allow two weeks for the compost to further decay then sow seeds in July or early August. This is an opportunity to try different varieties of leafy greens and brassicas. If you grew Swiss chard in the winter, try kale for a fall crop. If you grew broccoli earlier, why not plant cauliflower or kohlrabi for the fall? Do crop rotation within the greenhouse soil area. Don't plant the same category of plant in the same place. Some particular nutrients may have been depleted by the winter greenhouse crop. Move things around. Plant beets where there were brassicas, carrots where there were leafy greens, brassicas where there were lettuces, etc. All of these varieties will appreciate a cooling cover of burlap or shade cloth, so it may be best to leave the framing in place for supporting a shading material.

Seed starting pots on trays in the center square

Wire baskets filled with pots are a lightweight option for suspending from the greenhouse

Moving the Greenhouse

When fall frosts descend, and time to winterize the garden comes around, it's good to think about siting for the greenhouse and the winter crop of vegetables. If the greenhouse framing has been left in place through the summer, you have to decide whether to move the greenhouse to another eight foot square or whether to rotate the crops within the greenhouse area soil. If you choose a new site, it is not necessary to take the whole greenhouse apart to move it. You can remove the roof

Remove the roof supports and set them aside

Lift the wall posts one by one and move the framing to the new location

structure and then lift the wall studs out of the ground one by one to move it away. This will save a lot of time, but it does require at least two people carrying the frame at diagonal corners. If you do move the greenhouse to a new spot, imprint the soil with the pipes where they will be positioned. Move the greenhouse frame aside temporarily to deepen the post holes with a hammer and broomstick, old shovel handle, or ¾ inch dowel. Re-attach the roof rafters and cover with the plastic sheeting

Position the posts and imprint their positions on the soil

Pound a wooden dowel or broken broom handle with a hammer to deepen the post holes 4 or 5 inches

Reconnect the rafter trusses and the ridge pole supports. Cover with plastic

Prior greenhouse plan with five inches of snow

An Alternate Greenhouse Plan

I experimented with another way of building the greenhouse that would do a better job of shedding snow for locations that receive a lot of deep snowfalls each winter. It has a much steeper roofline, but is built using the same general instructions as the version put forth above. With this design, however, you will not need flexible pipe between the cross connectors and rafter connectors at each wall stud. Short lengths of pvc pipe will connect them given the angles with this plan.

The picture below shows the parts used. The connectors at the peak are 90° elbows and the connectors at the base of the rafters are 45°. The rafter lengths are approximately 50 inches. In order to keep the greenhouse closer to the ground, thus warmer and more stable, the wall stud lengths should be no more than four feet. Shorter walls won't make a difference while inside the greenhouse, since there's plenty of headroom at the central area. However, since ducking under a shorter crossbeam at the doorway may prove difficult for some people, I suggest holding up the front ridge pole with a pvc pipe sunk directly into the ground as shown below. Pass to one side of the pole to enter the geenhouse.

90° elbow connector

50 inch or so rafter length

45° connector

48 inch pipe lengths

ridge pole support in soil

Use the same general techniques for both versions of the greenhouse

Managing a Longer Growing Season

Whether you have space for only an 8 x 16 foot vegetable garden or can devote 8 x 24 feet, you can maximize the yield year round by planting at least three crops a year. Following are some diagrams of potential crop placement for 8 x 16 plots and 8 x 24 plots at three different times in a year: winter planting, late spring planting and summer planting. Additional diagrams show how crops can be rotated at the beginning of a second year.

Winter Planting

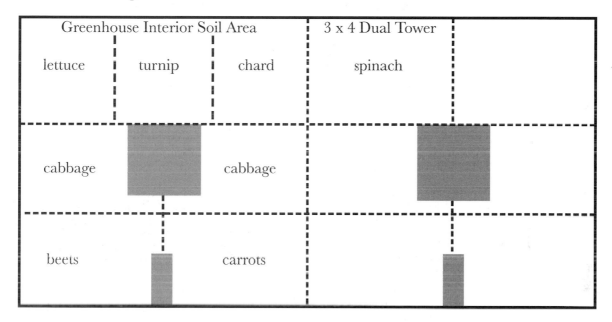

Late Spring Planting

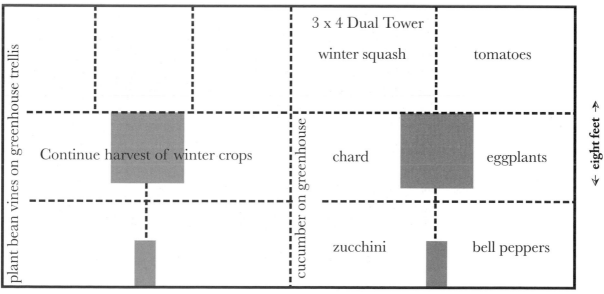

Summer Planting for Fall Harvest

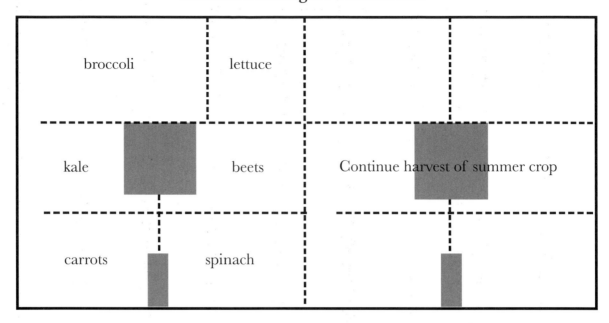

broccoli	lettuce	
kale	beets	Continue harvest of summer crop
carrots	spinach	

Greenhouse Moved in the Second Year

Winter Planting

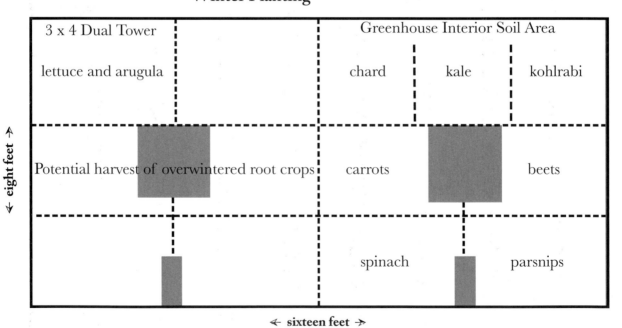

3 x 4 Dual Tower

lettuce and arugula

Greenhouse Interior Soil Area

chard   kale   kohlrabi

Potential harvest of overwintered root crops   carrots   beets

spinach   parsnips

← eight feet →

← sixteen feet →

Devoting a third 8 x 8 foot area to vegetable gardening will increase your yield and money savings by a lot without increasing your work load very much (except for the initial setup.) An 8 x 24 foot plot is highly recommended if you wish to provide most of your family's vegetables in a year.

Winter Planting

3' x 7' Dual Season Tower	Greenhouse Interior Soil Area			
sugar snap peas	lettuce	turnip	parsnip	
cabbage	cabbage		spinach	
	beets		carrots	

← twenty-four feet →

eight feet →

Late Spring Planting

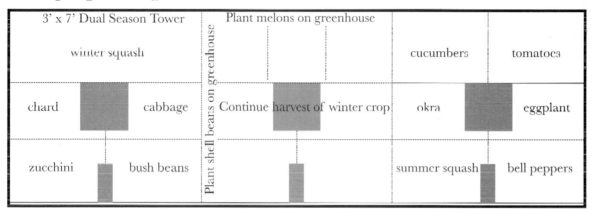

3' x 7' Dual Season Tower	Plant melons on greenhouse			
winter squash			cucumbers	tomatoes
chard / cabbage	Continue harvest of winter crop		okra / eggplant	
zucchini / bush beans			summer squash / bell peppers	

Plant shell beans on greenhouse

Summer Planting for Fall Harvest

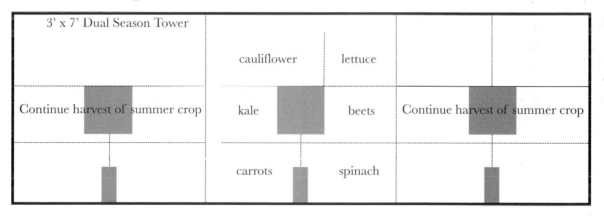

3' x 7' Dual Season Tower			
	cauliflower	lettuce	
Continue harvest of summer crop	kale	beets	Continue harvest of summer crop
	carrots	spinach	

Greenhouse Moved in the Second Year

Winter Planting

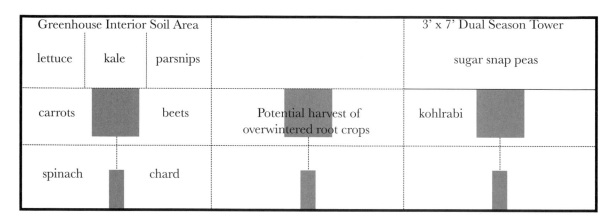

Greenhouse Interior Soil Area				3' x 7' Dual Season Tower	
lettuce	kale	parsnips		sugar snap peas	
carrots		beets	Potential harvest of overwintered root crops	kohlrabi	
spinach		chard			

5

Seed Saving

Growing Open Pollinated Seed Varieties

Saving seeds for future crops from the vegetable plants in the garden is an easy and satisfying way to eliminate some garden risks. In starting plants early, when there are extra seeds, you can simply start over if early seedlings succumb to frosts or predators. The money savings will add up as well, especially over the years, and seed saving promotes a rewarding sense of sustainability. You'll be amazed at how plentiful and bountiful is a plant's seed producing capacity; so much so that you'll usually have enough seed for a couple of years or to share with others.

It's generally easy to collect seeds. From the plants' side of the bargain, seeds are the goal — what they want us to use. Isn't it considerate to oblige them? Plants have evolved to reproduce themselves by a variety of means. Potatoes, for instance, most successfully make new plants through the tubers that we grow to eat. Strawberries put forth daughter plants. Most of our food producing plants reproduce themselves by making seeds. Seeds store the plant's genetic information in a dormant state until conditions are ripe for the seeds to sprout.

The production of seeds begins with the flower. At the point the flowers get pollinated, the flowers' ovaries begin to develop. We eat the flowers of some plants, for instance artichokes, broccoli, cauliflower, etc. We eat the seeds of others, such as: peas, beans, corn and other grains. We eat the fruits (ripened plant ovaries) of others, such as: pumpkins, tomatoes, peppers, zucchini, eggplant, okra, etc. These are all familiar seeds and fruits to most of us. We're less used to seeing the flowers and seeds of plants we eat the roots of, such as: beets, carrots, parsnips, or the leaves of, such as: lettuce, spinach, cabbage, etc. Most of the root crops are biennial plants that don't flower until the following spring.

In general, cross pollination between plants is beneficial for the long term health of the variety, but in a small garden it's better to limit cross pollination to two or so specimens of the same variety. If you grow a number of different kinds of tomatoes, for instance, the seeds produced may include the worst traits of the different strains. In a small space it will be impossible to control which and when plants are cross-pollinating. Another general tip is to choose the best looking, best performing plants or fruits for seed collecting. As for storing seeds, the biggest concern is to keep the seeds in a dry place. Paper envelopes are an excellent packaging for the seeds. You can also fold paper into a simple pouch with half a sheet of paper and a little tape.

Heirloom vegetable varieties that have produced well generation after generation are the best choices for seed collection. There are whole websites and mail order catalogs dedicated to preserving the diversity and availability of open pollinated seed types.

Different kinds of seeds require different collection methods, so the following guide is included to help you save seeds more easily and successfully.

Plants with Seeds We Eat: Peas, Beans, and Corn

These are very easy to collect. The seeds are large and visible without much extraneous material to winnow out. We tend to like to eat these foods when the seeds and or pods are immature, so the trick with peas, beans and corn is to remember to leave some good looking specimens to fully mature so you can harvest some large ripe seeds. At the same time, you do want to keep picking pea and bean pods to encourage the plants to make more of these delicious foods.

bean flowers

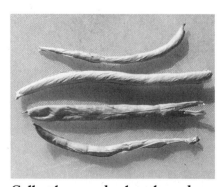

Collect bean seeds when the pods are dry and pale and the seeds are hard

I've found it a good strategy to keep an eye out for pods that have escaped my notice earlier and have become overly mature for pleasant eating. These are the pods I save for seed collecting. You'll know the seeds are ready when the pea or bean seeds are visibly bumpy in dried looking pods. Other creatures like to eat these too and it's all too likely that when you go to plant seeds the next year, you'll find little black critters in your envelopes and a hole in each seed. This infestation can be avoided by placing pea and bean seeds in a freezer for a few days (let's say 3 days) as soon as you harvest the pods.

Pea flowers

Pea pod dry and pale with visible seeds

Lettuces and Other Leafy Green Crops

For the small garden, I recommend leaf lettuce varieties instead of head lettuces. You'll be able to harvest many a salad by picking leaves from several different plants without having to uproot any of them. There will come a point in their growth when they start putting out taller stalks and the leaves become too bitter and leathery to eat. The lettuces are getting ready for seed production. At this stage, uproot all but two lettuce plants— the best two—and allow them to flower. The flower stalks produce sprays of small flowers. They are a little ragged looking but before too long you will see their seed pods maturing.

Multiple, small lettuce flowers

Fluffy ends of lettuce seed pods

113

Gently blow away the chaff

When you see the downy white fluff at the tips of the pods, your seed is ready for harvest. Collect the pods. Pull on the white fluffy tips to dislodge the seeds and let them fall onto a plate or towel. Blowing gently across the plate will help send the fluff airborn and away from the seed. Each plant will make more seeds than you'll need. Try to keep some from each plant for diversity, but don't feel you have to save every possible seed. Most of us are trained with the waste not want not dictum, but life is simply too short to feel responsible to every little seed your plants produce. If you collect enough for two years, however, you won't have to dedicate the space in the garden the following year.

Spinach

Spinach is odd because the plants are either male or female, but you will not be able to tell the difference until they start their reproductive cycles. Male plants put up tall stalks with fuzzy pollen bearing tips. Female spinach plants flower on the sides of the stalks. After releasing their pollen the male plants fizzle out and dry up. The female plants will have clusters of very hard seeds along the stalks. When mature, the clusters can be picked off the stalks and the seeds separated from one another by rubbing the clusters between thumb and fingers. Wear gloves because places on the spinach seeds have sharp points.

Male spinach plant sends up fuzzy pollen stalks

Female spinach plant bears flowers on its stems

Spinach seeds clustered on a stem

Cabbage and Kale

These are generally biennial seed flowering plants, and they don't necessarily survive the winter temperatures in all climates. If you want to collect seeds from cabbages and kale, you'll have to keep some heads alive over the winter in a greenhouse or surrounded by vessels of water and covered with a water-permeable cloth. Or start them in the greenhouse in winter for fall seed producing. When ready to seed, the plants will send up flowering stalks. Seeds are ready when the slender pouches circling the stalks become dry and the seeds hardened.

Plants with Flowers We Eat

Broccoli and cauliflower are the most common. The biggest challenge with collecting these seeds is resisting the temptation to eat the flowers. You have to wait awhile for the flowers and sometimes you wait quite awhile. So when you spot the head of flowers forming, especially if it's a big head forming, you're more likely to give in and eat it. With broccoli, sometimes side shoots can be left to mature into flowers. If winter is coming and you haven't saved any broccoli seeds, (or cauliflower) you can try to protect two plants over the winter as with cabbage above. These brassicas (also called cole crops that include broccoli, brussels sprouts, cabbage, cauliflower, kale, kohlrabi) have the capacity to hybridize, so only save seeds from one kind of brassica in a season. If you have cauliflower, broccoli and cabbage blooming at the same times, who knows what kind of seed you'll get. Try to save enough for a two or three year supply of any variety that you have isolated for seed saving. The seed collection is the same as for the cabbage and kale mentioned above.

Broccoli side shoots left to flower

Root Vegetables

Swiss Chard and Beet

We tend to think of chard as a leafy vegetable, since these are the parts we eat, but it is a close relative of beets and bears seeds biennially like other root crops. To winter over swiss chard for seed collection the next summer, it's generally enough in most climates to cover two chard plants with bags of composting materials. Bags with garden trimmings and bokashi are good. Bags of leaves which are usually plentiful in late

Swiss chard flowers on side shoots

Swiss chard seeds are hard and wrinkled

Beet seeds look very similar to swiss chard seeds

fall are also fine. The rotting material in the bag may warm the ground enough to keep the chard root alive until the next spring.

If your climate is too harsh for this simple treatment you can double up warming methods by using the bags of compost on top of the plants and surrounding this bag with cartons ¾ filled with water then covered with a cloth. If you have a greenhouse, some of the chard you plant in the winter will go to seed sometime before summer.

The same methods hold true for beets, as well. In the late spring, the beet and chard plants will send up a flower stalk with multiple branching side shoots. Seeds are formed on side shoots and the tip of the stalk. Swiss chard and beets make similar looking seeds that are generally hard and wrinkly when mature. They can cross pollinate, so allow only one or the other to flower each year..

Carrots

These root vegetables are also biennial. As with swiss chard and beets, if you're not starting carrots in the greenhouse in winter, these roots must be protected over the winter to secure the viability of the plants for spring blooming. Follow the suggestions cited above. These plants make different kinds of flowers than beets and chard. Carrot and parsnip flowers are very similar to the ubiquitous American wild flower, Queen Anne's Lace. Seeds will form on the top surface of the flowers. Wait until the flower seeds are visible on the surface of the dried brown flowers before harvesting the seeds. It will take a while for the seeds to be ready. Carrot seeds are small and dark. One carrot plant will make hundreds and hundreds. Extraneous chaff from the flowers will eventually have to be separated out.

Carrot flowers

Dried flower head laden with seeds

Parsnips

Parsnip flowers also resemble Queen Anne's lace, but they are yellow in color. One parsnip plant will produce copious round papery seeds. Pick them and allow them to dry for a few days before storing in a cool and dark place. Parsnip seeds have a short-lived viability and should be used within a year of harvesting. If you want to save seeds from your parsnips, it would be best to start them in a greenhouse in winter or in the fall and overwinter under plastic bags filled with composting material.

Parsnip has yellow flowers

Round papery parsnip seeds

Fruits

These include some of the most popular varieties of home grown foods: tomatoes, peppers, eggplants, cucumbers, squashes. The seeds are inside the juicy parts we eat. The main concern for collecting these seeds is waiting for ripe mature fruit before harvesting these seeds. Choose the biggest, most healthy looking specimens to save for seeds.

Cucumbers

Cucumber seeds are ready when the fruits look overripe and yellow skinned. Choose a mature one with good characteristics like size and straightness. Cucumber seeds benefit from fermentation of the seeds and surrounding pulp before collecting. Put the pulp into a jar with a little water and shake the jar a couple of times a day for three or four days. You may see mold forming, but that's quite all right. Extraneous material will float to the surface and mature seeds will sink to the bottom of the jar. Rinse the sunken seeds with water and allow them to dry on paper for a few days before packaging. All you will need is one good cucumber specimen for several years' worth of seeds.

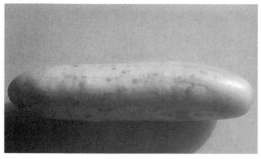

Collect seeds from pale overripe cucumbers

Seeds that fall to the bottom are viable

Winter Squash, Pumpkins and Melons

The nice thing about these fruits is that optimal seed collecting comes at the same time the vegetables are best to eat — as opposed to cucumbers and summer squashes that must be allowed to mature beyond the edible stage. Usually these melons and winter squashes are kept on the vine until after a frost when the vines become withered. These seeds are located in central cavities and can be easily scooped out. Like cucumbers, they benefit from a little fermentation for a few days. Separate the seeds from the surrounding fibrous material and place them in a jar with a little water. Shake the jar a couple of times a day for two or three days. Extraneous material will float to the surface and mature seeds will sink to the bottom of the jar. Rinse the seeds with water and allow them to dry on paper for a few days before packaging.

Female squash flower with tiny fruit attached

Seeds that fall to the bottom are viable

Tomatoes

Tomato seeds are encased in gelatinous packages that keep the seeds from sprouting inside the fruit. Tomato seeds must be fermented to break open this casing. Collect these gelatinous seed pouches and put them in a jar for a few days. When you see mold forming on the pulp, look for mature seeds on the bottom of the jar. Rinse the seeds and allow them to dry on paper for a few days before storing.

Tomato flowers

Dislodge the seed pouches

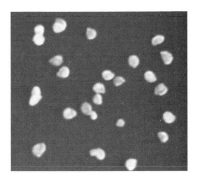

**Small off-white
tomato seeds**

Peppers

Pepper seeds are all found in a dry inner cavity and are easy to collect. Choose the best, most mature specimens. If the pepper has turned red (or yellow, purple orange, depending on the variety) and the skin is a little wrinkled the seeds will be ready. Discard any discolored or misshapen seeds. Allow them to dry thoroughly before storing.

Pepper flowers

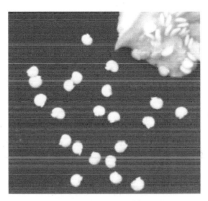

**Pepper seeds cluster inside
under the stem**

Zucchini

Cut open a fully mature zucchini and scoop out some seeds. Separate the seeds from the pulp and allow them to soak overnight in a jar of water. Dry on paper for a week or so until completely dry.

Zucchini seeds

Eggplant

Unless the eggplant is fully mature, you may have trouble even seeing the seeds, so allow one choice specimen to become very ripe. Scoop out some pulp from the center bottom of the eggplant. Break up the pulp with your fingers and soak it all in a jar of water overnight.

Separate out the seeds and allow them to soak another day or so to remove the coating on each seed. Allow them to dry on paper for a week or so until completely dry, then store in a cool place.

Eggplant flowers

Select an overripe fruit

Small off-white seeds

Okra

Wait until a pod has become very dried and woody before collecting the seeds. Overlooked pods that have grown too big to eat are good candidates. Simply crush a pod and the large round seeds will spill out.

Okra flowers

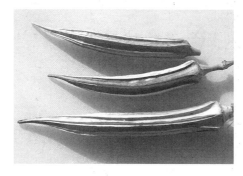

Dried okra pods

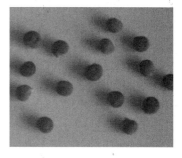

Hard round okra seeds

Onion

Onion plants will freely self-sow in the surrounding soil after the flowers mature into clusters of black seeds. Sprouts transplant very easily, so allowing onions to sprout and then moving them the next spring is a good strategy for propagation in most U.S. climates.

Onion flowers

Clusters of round black seeds

Onions sprouting in the bed

Seed Storage Life

As mentioned earlier, collecting seed for multiple years will help to save future garden space during those transitional times between crop harvest and the next sowing. Plants kept for seed production definitely take up space that could be devoted to new plants. Following is a guide to how long various kinds of seeds can last to help you plan seed saving for some years ahead.

Short Storage Life (1-2 years) – Onion, Corn, Pepper, Parsnip
Medium Storage Life (3-4 years) – Bean, Broccoli, Carrot, Pea
Long Storage Life (5+ years) – Cabbage, Radish, Cucumber,
Eggplant, Lettuce, Melon, Pumpkin, Squash, Tomato

As a final word of advice, if you are allowing a few plants in the greenhouse area to go to seed, select specimens that are growing close to the greenhouse's wall studs for staking and tying up the seed laden plants.

6

Some Common Garden Concerns

One of the great conditions of living in my high dry climate is the lack of insect pests I see in the garden. I do have snails to discourage and some grasshoppers in late summer, but these present nothing like the problems I used to have when we lived in wetter parts of the country. Nowadays, there are various non-poisonous ways to safeguard vegetable gardens from insects and other pests, including products that are not harmful to people, the living creatures in the soil, or beneficial insects. However, these products do kill the insects that actually ingest the vegetable plants. There are many online sources of information about these non-toxic pest control products. In this chapter I will be presenting only the non-lethal pest control measures that I use.

Effective Microorganisms as Insect Deterrent

The same EM 1 introduced in chapter two for making the bokashi composting medium can also be used to make a safe, and effective insect repellent to be sprayed on plant leaves. Following is an effective formula using EM1 straight out of the bottle. It does not have to be activated beforehand as in making bokashi. This treatment will have to be repeated frequently to discourage persistent insects.

How to Make the EM Repellent

This mix will make a non-toxic, chemical free insect repellent. It can be used to prevent pest and disease problems in the garden. It acts by creating a disguising barrier around plants thereby protecting them from insects. The mix can be enhanced with pungent herbs such as garlic, onion, or hot pepper to add discouraging scents to the plants. These additional herbal ingredients are chopped or mashed prior to inclusion in the mixture.

The Ingredients

1 ⅓ cups warm water (chlorine free)

3 tbs molasses

3 tbs natural vinegar

3 tbs whiskey or ethyl alcohol

3 tbs EM liquid concentrate

3 tbs chopped garlic cloves and or other pungent herbs

Select a suitable sized container for mixing, some bottles or jars with caps for storage, and a funnel. Add the molasses to the warm water and stir until thoroughly mixed. Then add the vinegar, whiskey and EM concentrate. Pour the mix into a bottle and add small quantities of chopped garlic and/or other pungent herbs. Seal as tightly as possible and leave in a warm dark place. Release any gas produced at least twice daily by opening the cap. The solution is ready for use when the production of gas has stopped and it smells distinctly potent. The mix can be stored in a dark cool place for up to three months (but not in a refrigerator). Strain out the garlic bits, etc. before storing.

Using the EM Repellent Mix

Dilute one tablespoon of the mix in a quart of water in a spray bottle and spray enough of the mix to wet the crop. Spraying can begin at seed germination or planting and certainly before pests and diseases can be seen. After a season or two of vegetable gardening, you will know what pests to expect. If an attack occurs, use up to two tablespoons of solution in a quart of water. Spray weekly either in the morning or after heavy rains for best results.

Compost Tea Repellent

The compost tea formula introduced in chapter two can also be used as a spray medium for the pungent oils described above, such as garlic, to discourage insects and other pests. When making compost tea as a fertilizer, you can put aside a quantity to be used as a foliar spray infused with pungent oils. Add a few tablespoons of chopped garlic and/or hot peppers to a quart of compost tea and allow the solution to steep for a day or so. Spray on plants to dicourage pests as well as feed the plants through its leaves.

To avoid muscle fatigue while spraying the remedies above, use a pump spray bottle that allows the contents to be under slight pressure.

Pressurized plastic spray bottle

Discouraging Snails and Slugs

Since snails are the most ubiquitous raiders of my vegetable patch, I have experimented with quite a few ideas for discouraging them. I have attached copper flashing to the wood surrounding the garden, since, supposedly, snails can't handle coming in contact with copper, which chemically reacts with their skin. Yet, the snails do crawl across the copper, so it's not totally effective. I also tried attaching carpet tack strips to the wooden border to no avail. I once had the idea to construct a moat around the garden using four inch flexible drain pipe bisected lengthwise and arranged to form a channel around the garden that could be sealed with silicone and filled with water. I never really tried this idea, yet perhaps it could work, since I'm pretty sure that snails can't swim.

My current snail and slug strategy is to start the season early by sowing seeds in the greenhouse before the slugs and snails are active. Once plants are of sufficient size they can withstand a little nibbling, and the snails and slugs can simply be moved away when found. A daily snail patrol, especially in the evening and during wet weather, can steadily deecrease their numbers You can pick up snails by the shell and slugs can be nudged onto a piece of cardboard to be moved. Spraying the plants with the solutions described above can also dampen their enthusiasm for the plants that continually smell like garlic or onion, etc. (I never see snails eating my onion plants.)

The time I have the worst trouble with these creatures is when sowing in summer for the fall crop. I have lost all my seedlings to these voracious little competitors during my plantings in July. In the summer season, I now construct shallow cages of hardware cloth (metal screening material) to place over newly seeded areas.

The Hardware Cloth Seedling Cage

Cut and stretch out a length of hardware cloth. Then use a hammer and 2 x 4 to mark off and pre-bend lines for a four inch skirt all around

124

Bend with your fingers on one side of the cage

Cut at the corner to make a box fold

Fold the next side and fix the corner working all the way around the cage

When the cage is constructed, settle it in the soil area to be protected

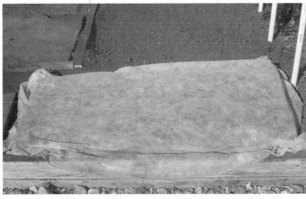

Cover with a porous garden cloth to keep out the tiniest invaders

Seal the edges of the cloth with soil

I've also had some success with simply covering seeded areas with a porous garden cloth that is then sealed to the ground by piling soil over its edges. As far as I know, snails and slugs don't burrow much. The cloth on the ground keeps out pests but somewhat discourages the plant growth as well.

Garden cloth is laid directly on the ground as a barrier to garden pests

For this reason, I prefer to construct the box like cages and cover these with garden cloth, since baby snails and slugs start out pretty small. The cages can be removed when plants are bigger and the hardware cloth can be flattened and stored for later use.

Water

The amount of watering you'll need to keep your vegetables healthy will depend entirely on your local climate conditions. Most summers in my locale, we get scarcely a drop of rain from June through August, and frequent watering is essential for our plants. If you have little rainfall in your area, it might be worthwhile to install an automatic watering system to regularly and easily fulfill your garden's water needs. If you have to do a lot of hand watering, your garden is going to seem like a lot of work! There are even battery run, self-timing systems of soaker hoses or above ground sprinklers that are easy to install. Automatic watering allows you to schedule watering sessions in early morning hours when there's less waste of water through evaporation. An outdoor water spigot will be essential for these automatic systems.

Rain Barrels

A rain barrel on a downspout can be an easy way to save water for your plants. Rainwater can be put to use immediately when working with microorganisms in making compost tea. Even a short burst of rainfall collected from a significant section of roof goes a long way toward filling a fifty-gallon drum. An estimation of rainwater collection is 0.6 gallons per square foot of roof per inch of rainfall. A 1,000 square foot roof that received a half inch of rain would provide approximately 300 gallons of rainwater. Plants love rainwater. It is naturally soft water without any minerals, chlorine, fluoride, or other chemicals, which doesn't hold true for many municipal water sources. On the subject of municipalities, I have heard that there are some jurisdictions that forbid their citizens personal rainwater collection, so it might be worth a check with local authorities before going ahead with a rain barrel.

You can use different kinds of barrels for water collection. Plastic is nice, but metal will also work. It doesn't have to start out with a spigot. You can install a spigot yourself. The instructions for tapping a rain barrel are the same as put forth in chapter two for tapping the bokashi bucket. You just need a drill bit that is $1/8$ th inch larger than the diameter of the tap or spigot. If you do wish to tap a rain barrel, acquire a spigot/faucet with a threaded end that a garden hose can screw on for easier watering.

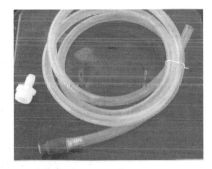

Emergency siphon starter

It is not necessary to tap the barrel, though. You can check with beer making supply sources for a manual barrel pump. I use an emergency siphon device to drain the barrel. The most important factor is that the barrel be clean and without toxic residues from previous storage jobs.

Connecting a rain barrel to a downspout doesn't have to be difficult or a permanent placement. Many hardware stores carry flexible adaptors of accordion folded plastic that provide a lot of flexibility to where you place the rain barrel. The flexing section can be angled toward the rain barrel or be a straight shot through the full downspout for winter use or other times you don't want the rain barrel to be connected. The rain barrel can even be situated around the corner from the downspout. Between the flexible section and extra pieces of downspout, many arrangements are possible for the rain barrel/downspout connection. The hardest part is cutting a section out of the existing downspout with a saw that can cut through metal.

Flexible adaptor can connect to a rain barrel or complete the downspout

Placement

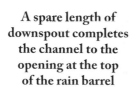

Raised on a platform

Given some choice, the first consideration for locating the rain barrel is volume of water catchment. If possible, choose the downspout that drains the largest section of roof — hence receives the most rain. Another consideration is height above the ground level of the vegetable patch. If the rain barrel can be situated higher, the water can flow more easily through a hose connected to a spigot. It will also be easier to start a siphon when the base of the barrel is higher than ground level. Building a platform of cement blocks, concrete wall blocks or bricks to raise the rain barrel is definitely recommended. Shade is also desirable to keep water cooler, thus less suitable for incubating organisms that can grow on debris collected in the barrel.

How to Set Up a Rainbarrel

Cut out a section of the downspout

Attach the adaptor to the downspout

A spare length of downspout completes the channel to the opening at the top of the rain barrel

Use a very fine mesh screen that more than completely covers the opening to the barrel to filter debris. I managed to find material for screens in a local thrift shop by taking apart a mesh paper organizing folder I found on a thrift shop shelf. It's possible that a kitchen sink strainer will work, but because of its small diameter, it may fill up too quickly with debris from the gutters.

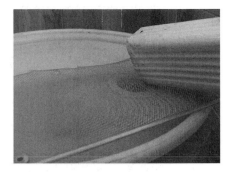

**Screening over the opening
to keep out debris**

Structuring Water

In the last few decades, amazing properties of water have been and still are being discovered. Water can exist in various molecular arrangements, and some arrangments provide greater support for life processes than others. Many people are already familiar with the work of Japanese scientist Masaru Emoto who demonstrated the almost miraculous property of water to respond to human thoughts. In his tests, Emoto mentally imprinted emotions in glasses of water and then froze the water to examine the effects. Beautiful crystal arrangements appeared in ice when positive emotions were expressed, whereas negative emotions showed up as chaotic, ungraceful looking ice.

There are things you can do with your rain barrel to enhance the molecular structure of the rainwater and make it more beneficial for your plants and other living organisms. In structured water the molecules are hexagonal and orderly. One study done at the University of Georgia showed that structured water could be found around healthy cells, but the water surrounding all diseased cells was unstructured. There have also been studies showing that crops require between ten to thirty percent less water when irrigated with structured water.

Rainwater can be channeled to enhance structure in the water in a couple of different ways. One way is to include some egg-sized pebbles somewhere in the delivery ducting to the rain barrel. This is how water in nature becomes structured while flowing over rocks in streams. The rocks can also filter out some debris as well. Just make sure the rocks will still allow enough flow.

Another way to structure water is to band magnets around the downspout and other ducts, so the water flows through a magnetic field. Once these options are set up, the structuring takes place passively. There's nothing more to do, so there isn't much to lose in trying out these ideas. I have to confess that I haven't really tested these ideas in any systematic, controlled study. However, some tests I ran to see how plants fared when fed water energized by sun sound vibrations showed very positive effects. So water might be more easily influenced than we generally think is possible. As for imprinting with thoughts ala Masaru Emoto, well, I'm fairly certain you will love your garden and all your plants.

Adding Rocks to the Water Course

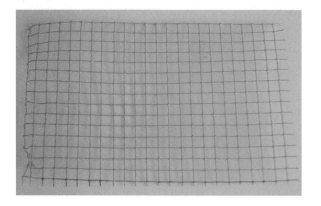

Cut a 6 x 4 inch section of hardware cloth or other metal screening

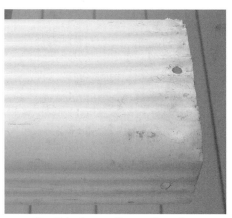

Drill holes on four sides of a length of downspout

Fold the screen over the downspout

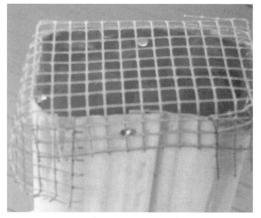

Cut the screen at the corners to fold over all sides of the downspout

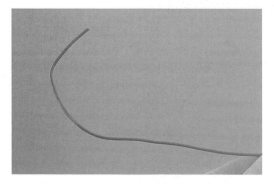

Cut a two or three inch piece of wire

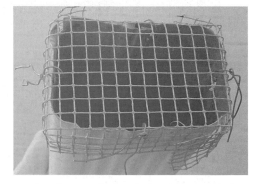

Wrap the wire around the screen and the holes in the downspout

**Insert rounded egg-sized rocks
into the final length of downspout
and place it over the hole
in the top of the barrel**

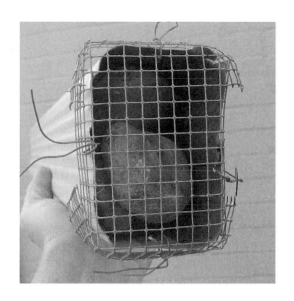

Structuring Water with a Magnetic Field

Creating a magnetic field in the water course is as simple as placing magnets in opposition on all four sides of the downspout. The magnets can be placed at the end of the course as shown here, or elsewhere along the channel. Downspouts are usually made of aluminum, which magnets will not stick to, so they will have to be banded on.

I'm offering these ideas here without knowing if they really work because they're easy and inexpensive to accomplish. If they do help plants grow better and with less water, the efforts will be well worth it.

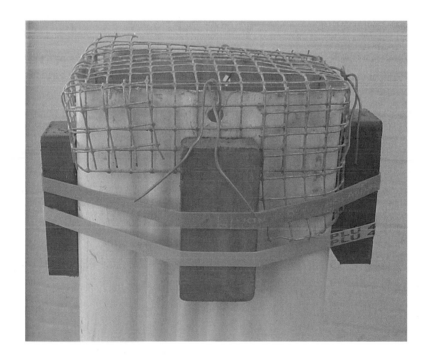

**Rubber bands hold magnets
in place on a length
of aluminum downspout**

Burying Watering Vessels

One way to conserve water is by watering deeply into the soil through buried containers that bring water down to the roots. This method avoids a lot of evaporation that occurs when we sprinkle water on the surface. I don't recommend this option for most vegetable gardeners. However, if watering is a problem, for instance, if you have no nearby outdoor water source, and rain is not plentiful, it may be worthwhile to sacrifice some vegetable growing space and bury a grid of 2 liter plastic bottles as watering vessels placed every two feet or so.

This will have to be planned ahead at the very beginning of the vegetable patch because much soil will have to be displaced to put this grid in place. You'll want to plant seeds around these buried bottles after they are in place rather than disturbing plants after the fact.

You'll need the 2 liter bottles as well as their lids. Using a pin, pierce the plastic bottle in a symmetrical pattern in the following manner. Place four holes in a vertical line near the base about ¾ of an inch apart. Rotate the bottle a quarter turn and make another vertical line of four pinholes, rotate another quarter turn and repeat, then add a fourth vertical line of four pinholes. Bury the bottle up to the neck, fill with water and screw on the cap. The water will slowly release to moisten soil deep within the bed. You'll probably only have to water every three days using this method.

Make pin hole leaks above the base on four sides of a plastic bottle. Heating the pin in a flame will make piercing easier

This way of watering is very good for established plants, however, it will not be sufficient for seed sprouting. The top surface of the soil will have to be moistened to encourage germination of seeds. Often spring rains are enough, but other means to keep the surface of the soil moist will have to employed when you want seeds to sprout.

I have found this method of watering to be helpful for irrigating deeply in soil-less raised beds, thus reducing the amount of water generally needed for these beds that heat up quickly and evaporate a lot of water. If you have any raised beds, try this simple expedient for saving water.

Three buried 2 liter plastic bottles in a 3 x 6 foot raised bed

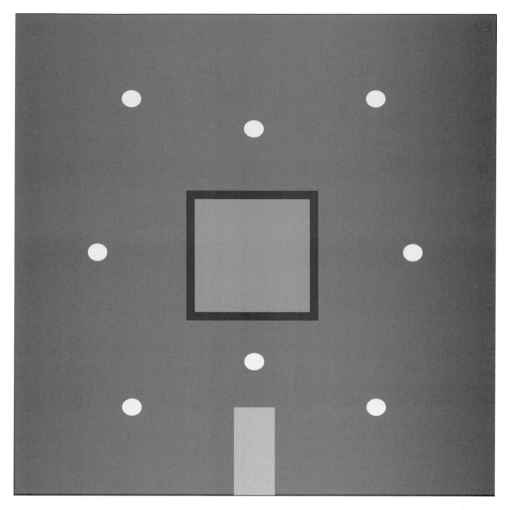

A Grid of Buried Bottles in an 8 x 8 foot Garden Bed

7

Making Food Last

The aim of this book is to eat fresh vegetables as long as possible throughout the year. Storage of excess garden produce is not likely to be a very time consuming task with small spaces, especially with an 8 x 16 foot plot. But if you do have a bumper crop that you need to move out of the garden — fall is usually the time when this happens — there are three options for food storage: canning, freezing and drying.

I have my definite preferences for how to store different vegetables and fruits. I always use a lot of canned tomatoes throughout the year and with concerns about the plastics that are used for lining the insides of commercially packed foods, I like to can my own. However, having some sundried tomatoes months later is desirable as well. This section of the book is not meant to be a comprehensive guide to food storage, but rather a personal account of suitable ways to make the food in your garden last longer. There are many books and sources of online information about canning, freezing and drying. My most unique offering in this chapter is showing how to make a simple, effective solar food drying arrangement that works very well to dry food with no power source other than the sun.

One of the saddest moments for the vegetable gardener is hearing news of an impending frost when tomato vines are still loaded with green tomatoes. After all, how many fried green tomatoes can a family eat? Since doing this intensive gardening, I've learned not to completely despair on these chilly fall nights. Many of these late tomatoes will eventually ripen if left out in bowls at room temperature. If the frost will only be light, its possible to preserve tomato plants by covering them with cloth or plastic overnight. If the temperatures are really going to dip, then its best to harvest all the tomatoes and give them a chance to ripen. I have been so very pleased with the number of these tomatoes that do eventually turn red. Last fall we were eating our tomatoes until the end of November.

Canning

In 1974, chemists at the National Food Processors Association analyzed the contents of 100 year old canned foods that came from the stores of an old steamboat. They found that, although the contents no longer looked appealing, the foods were as safe to eat as the day they had been canned. If you're looking for the longest shelf life, canning is probably the best option for food storage.

Traditional pot for canning

Many vegetables don't have enough acidity to be safely canned using the simple boiling water bath method. If canning is your top choice for food preservation, then I suggest purchasing and learning how to use a pressure cooker for canning. Tomatoes, however, with the addition of some acidic substance like lemon juice or vinegar can be safely preserved by hot water bath canning methods. The most challenging part of processing the tomatoes is removing their skins. A few years ago I decided I would remove the skins upon opening my canned tomatoes, thus only investing a minute or two while cooking. Simply place a colander on top of a bowl; pour tomatoes into the colander; remove the skins; and collect the juice from the bowl. This saves a lot of time in the tomato canning process. There's also no reason to remove the seeds. It's been discovered that the most tomato-ey flavored parts of the tomato are the gelatinous pouches around the seeds. Wouldn't want to lose that flavor by throwing the seeds away.

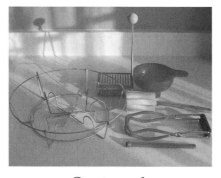

Canning tools

Anything pickled in vinegar, such as: cucumbers, okra, beets, etc. can also be safely canned in a hot water bath. If you have a lot of cucumbers, the only way to store them is to pickle them. I have discovered that decent pickles can be made from regular slicing cucumbers if you soak the whole cucumbers in an ice water bath overnight before pickling.

Always scrupulously follow safe canning directions and use fresh canning lids when preserving food in this way. Harmful, even life-threatening, bacteria can grow in carelessly canned foods.

Freezing

Freezing is a good choice for many vegetables, though the shelf life of frozen food has limits. Most fruits and vegetables last about six to eight months when home frozen. However, tomatoes and peppers last only three months or so. If you plant a garden year after year, then six months to a year of storage is probably a long enough storage time.

I find that some of the best foods to freeze are greens that you would normally serve steamed or boiled. Greens, such as spinach, swiss chard, turnip greens, etc. are usually served with a somewhat watery consistency anyway. To freeze these greens remove the stems and blanch the leaves in boiling water for a minute then transfer to an ice water bath for a minute, drain well, place in plastic freezer bags and expel as much air out of the bag as you can.

Peppers are remarkably easy to freeze. Cut peppers in half, remove the seeds and stem, and place pepper halves in a single layer on a tray in the freezer for several hours before placing them in plastic freezer bags..

Tomatoes are even easier to freeze. Pop them in freezer bags skins and all. The skins will come off easily when they're placed in boiling water for a few minutes and allowed to cool a bit.

Most Vegetables Can Be Frozen by the Following Steps:

1. Dice or slice the vegetables
2. Blanch in boiling water
3. Immerse in ice water
4. Drain thoroughly
5. Spread out on a tray in a single layer for an hour or so
6. Place in freezer bags
7. Expel as much air as possible.

The amount of time to blanch in boiling water depends upon the vegetable and the size of the pieces. Generally two or three minutes is enough. Following are some specific guidelines.

Blanching/Icing Times for Common Vegetables

Beans — 2 minutes.
Broccoli, Brussels sprouts, and Cauliflower florets — 3 minutes
Cabbage — 2 minutes.
Carrot slices — 3 minutes
Parsnip slices — 2 minutes
Peas and snow peas — 1 minute
Zucchini can be steamed for a minute then placed directly in freezer bags.
Some vegetables, namely, beets and eggplants have to be sliced and fully cooked before freezing.

Dehydrating

Food drying removes most of the moisture from foods while retaining much of the nutritional value and flavor. Fruits typically contain about 75 percent moisture when fresh, and should be dehydrated to a 20 percent moisture level, the point at which they become dried yet pliant. It is acceptable for fruits to be dried to this level rather than a lower moisture level because the natural sugars and acids in fruit act as an added preservative. Vegetables must be dehydrated to a moisture level around 5 percent, the point at which they become stiff and breakable.

Most of the work of food drying is done by the sun, or whatever electric powered drying device used. There is initial work in slicing the vegetables before drying and also in turning the pieces over to expose all surfaces to the source of warm air. The thickness of the slices will influence the time needed for drying. Less thick means faster drying. However, thinner slices will take up more surface area on the drying rack, so the whole process of drying a quantity of food may not be speedier in cutting thinner slices. Also thinner slices can be harder to handle and more easily broken when dried.

Foods to Directly Dry:

Broccoli slices

Carrot slices

Eggplant slices

Garlic halves (remove sprout in the middle first)

Leek slices

Okra slices

Onion bits

Pepper slices

Spinach leaves

Swiss chard (stems removed)

Tomato slices or halves of small tomatoes

Zucchini slices

Vegetables to Blanch in Boiling Water for a Minute Before Drying

Bussels sprouts slices

Cabbage leaves

Parsnip slices

Peas

Summer squash slices

Green beans should be blanched a minute and immersed in an ice bath before drying.

Beets should be fully cooked before drying.

Potatoes need to be soaked in a lemon juice and water solution before drying

Store dried vegetables in a clean, dry, airtight container, in a cool, dark location.

Shelf Life of Home Dried Foods

Home dried foods generally have a shelf life of six months to year, which is similar to home frozen foods. However, storage conditions have a greater impact on dried foods. Light, temperature and exposure to oxygen will all have their effect on the stored goods.

If you store your dried food at a room temperature of about seventy degrees, the food should last about a year. Store it at sixty degrees and the food can last two years. At eighty degrees, the food will last about six months. For every ten degrees lower temperature, you can double the shelf life of your dried foods. So if you have a basement, consider keeping your food storage containers in the coolness below ground level.

The lower light level in basements is also good for storage, since light can cause dried foods to discolor and eventually spoil. It's also been demonstrated that light eventually breaks down fats and proteins as well as vitamins in the food.

The other factor limiting the shelf life of dried foods is oxygen. The presence of oxygen in the food container will eventually cause the foods to break down resulting in off flavors and eventual spoilage. The more airtight the container, the longer your home dried food will last.

I usually keep foods I dry in plastic bags in the refrigerator. I've been able to eat sun dried tomatoes a year later when stored in the cold dark of the refrigerator shelves.

Oven roasting pan with slotted tray

How to Make a Simple Solar Food Dryer

On a really hot summer day when temperatures hover around 100 degrees, all you really need to do for dehydrating food is place slices on an oven roasting tray and move it all into the sunshine. A pan that has a slotted top tray with a catchment basin beneath is especially good.

The solar dryer I designed will help with food drying tasks later in the year when air temperatures are lower. The design offered below is very inexpensive to make. It is designed to accomodate the kind of roasting tray/pans described above that are generally dark in color, thus more heat absorbent. The pan is the central feature and the solar drying components are built around it. If you don't already own an oven roasting pan, keep an eye out for one at yard sales and thrift shops.

You will need:

A dark colored roasting pan
One cardboard box at least as large as the pan.
Aluminum foil
Tape

Find a box the pan can fit in

Measure 3 inches from the bottom of the box

Measure 1 inch from the bottom of the box
on the other end of the box

Draw a line between the two marks
to create an angled line.
Then repeat these steps on the
opposite side of the box

Draw a line from the one inch mark on one end
to the one inch mark on the other end.
Draw a line connecting the three inch marks on
the opposite side

Cut on all the marked lines to create
a sloped box platform

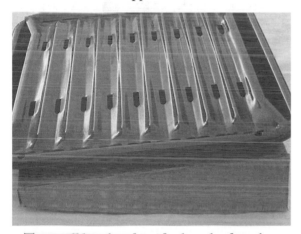

These will be placed inside the solar dryer box

Insert the sloped base into
the leftover top of the box

Cut lengths of aluminum foil for each box flap
that are longer than the flap so that they overlap the
neighboring flaps. Fold the foil lengths over the
box flaps. Hold them in place temporarily
with clips. Foil can be glued to the flaps if desired-
But this is not necessary

Turn the box on its side and bring
all the foil out to the side at a corner.
Smooth it out and
draw a 45° angle on the foil.

Cut on the marked line

Ready to be folded

Fold the foil inward toward the box corner
keeping the 45° angle

Tape the folded corner
Construct the other corners the same way

Tape the foil on the flaps
to the inside of the box

Place the roasting pan inside

Although there are several steps to making this solar dryer, they can all be accomplished in just a few minutes, so making it should take much less than an hour. Use this solar dryer on sunny days when you have garden produce you wish to dehydrate. You can test its temperature with a thermometer and adjust the box for maximum sun exposure if the temperature falls below 100 degrees.

This box can also be used for cooking if you use a dark colored cooking pot to absorb the sunlight. Black enamel-ware pots are good choices. You will also need to put your pot inside an oven roasting bag to maintain the higher temperatures needed to cook food.

If you wish to do a lot of solar cooking, you may want to construct a box with more reflective power by gluing higher pieces of cardboard onto the box flaps. Making sure you have enough foil to overlap the corners, smoothly glue the foil to these extended flaps. Construct the corners using the same method as for the solar dehydrator.

About the Author

Author and inventor Margaret Park has been growing vegetables for more than thirty years in backyards across the country. With her latest move to a house near downtown Salt Lake City, and her tiniest yard ever, she had to reinvent her approach to growing vegetables. Now she grows more vegetables in an 8 x 24 foot patch than she used to get out of a garden three times that size.

After completely rethinking the relationship of cultivation to working space she came up with the Center Square plan that maximizes the space for plant cultivation. She also learned the benefits of microorganisms for building soil and tested the space-and-time-saving bokashi composting methods explained in this book. The strong and durable plant towers and trellises introduced here are her own innovations that have many advantages, including ease of assembly and disassembly. She also designed the portable greenhouse which can even be used off-season as a trellis support. Many of the other ideas in this book are also her unique and successful innovations, the fruit of years of experimentation and happy gardening.

She is also the author of four children's books: *Crab-bags And Other Bean Beings; A Fish That's A Box; Harvey, Rosie and Ralph;* and *Now for My Next Number!*

Follow Margaret Park on her **Center Square Gardens** Facebook page, she's always coming up with fresh new ideas for greater garden yields and more sustainable living.